Introduction To Australian Law

Commentary From An Underqualified Undergrad

...

With Additions From A Law Graduate

...

& Further Additions From A Solicitor Who Does Not Practice Law But Practices Medicine Instead

Dr Stephen George Prorellis

This edition is for Thalia,

Who keeps me on my toes every single day

Disclaimer: This is not an attempt to give legal advice, nor is it suited for that role. If you seek legal advice, a qualified (and practicing) lawyer would be able to address your needs, and this book can't.

My thanks also to the University of New South Wales Law School and all the dedicated teachers therein. You taught me everything I know about the law. This book is based upon that knowledge which you have handed down to me and would not have been possible without your tutelage.

Thanks also for some of the best years of my life……..and also for putting me in the same class as my future wife

Table of Contents

Settlement of Australia	*11*
Separation of Powers	*16*
Rights Protection	*22*
Administrative Law	*32*
Criminal Law	*43*
Contract Law	*80*
Equity	*106*
Torts	*155*
Government	*179*

PRELUDE – AN UNBROKEN CHAIN

The Western legal tradition is a long one – going back to antiquity. The legal codes of the ancient world provide the bedrock foundations upon which our systems are built. There are, of course, changes which have been made over the long years. Some fundamental principles remain though, such as in the recognition that the law must reflect nature – the so-called *natural law*. An example here can be found in the law regarding adoption. Going back to the old Roman legal codes, one could not legally adopt someone younger than themselves. Allowing such a thing would be an afront to the natural order of the world and was hence disallowed.

If one takes the time to look at the family law arrangements around the Western world, we still have the very same (or very similar) laws to ban such unnatural adoptions. Similarly, rules of inheritance have been developed to mirror the natural order of things. If one dies intestate (without a will), the property will generally flow by default to the nearest kin before going to relations more distant.

That is not to say that the law has always been developed with a view towards the laws of nature. Sometimes very explicit deviations were created in man-made legal codes. The most obvious deviation, and the one that has created the largest ripples throughout world history, must be slavery.

The institution is, of course, an ancient one. Every single human society on earth has practiced it at some point. And every single race has equally been its victim. The Roman legal codes are perhaps the most interesting read on the subject. Justinian's Code, for example, makes explicit that the institution of slavery is an afront to the laws of nature – and yet the laws of man allow it.

What is intriguing, however, is that the Western legal tradition slowly evolved to end the institution – gradually having the laws of man mirror the laws of nature. We start with the presumption that babes of slave mothers are born free (in certain circumstances, for example, if at any point during the pregnancy, the mother was a free woman) within the Roman law.

We then move towards ever more enlightened ideas of human dignity. *Somersett's Case*, for example, has perhaps my favourite line in any judgment every written.

The case revolved around a slave that was taken to England by his owner. The slave, James Somersett, escaped. He was then baptised, and his godparents made an application to have him freed under *habeas corpus*.

The most pivotal paragraph in the judgment is just beautiful.

Lord Mansfield's ruling is a true now as it was back then,

'The State of Slavery, is of such a nature, that it is incapable of being introduced on any reasons; moral or political, but only introduced by positive law. Which continues to preserve its force long after the reasons, occasions, and time itself from whence it was created is erased from memory. It is so odious that nothing can be suffered to support it - but positive law. Whatever inconveniences, therefore, may follow from this decision, I cannot say this case is allowed, or approved, by the laws of England - and therefore the black must be discharged.'[1]

We move from this case towards the abolition debates of the next century. William Wilberforce, arguably the most influential politician in this area, who spearheaded the ending of slavery in the British Empire, similarly stated before the Commons.

'Let us not despair, this is a blessed cause, and success ere long - will crown all our exertions. Already we have gained a victory, we have obtained, for these poor creatures, the recognition of their human nature, which, for a long while was most shamefully denied. This is the first fruits for our efforts, let us persevere and triumph will be complete. Never, never, will we desist until we have wiped away this scandal from the Christian name and released ourselves from the load of guilt under which, we at present labour, and extinguished every trace of this bloody traffic, of which our posterity; looking back to the history in these enlightened times, will scarcely believe that it has been suffered to exist for so long a disgrace and dishonour to this country.'

Inexorably, the debate then turned decidedly in favour of the abolitionists and culminated with the *Slavery Abolition Act*.[2] Legislation which ended, forever, the scourge of slavery in the British Empire (with some exceptions, for complicated reasons, in the subcontinent – these exceptions would then be dealt with in relatively short order).

The passage of the bill serves as a masterclass in messy political compromise. The wealthy slave owners complained, of course, but the Bill's passage was secured by essentially paying them the value of their former chattel. That is, to secure the freedom of almost every slave in

---

[1] *Somerset v Stewart* (1772) 98 ER 499 (Lord Mansfield).
[2] *Slavery Abolition Act 1833*, 3 & 4 Will 4, c 73.

the British Empire, the government had to pay nearly half of its annual revenue to bribe their former owners into submission.

If that wasn't enough, the British government then leveraged its worldwide empire and its navy, that unambiguously ruled the waves, to enforce its abolitionist movement on the entire world. The Royal Navy, through the West Africa Squadron, ran a century long campaign to ensure that the global slave trade was ended. Gradually, and with great expense of blood and treasure (these naval postings were some of the most dangerous of the era), abolition became the norm instead of the exception. The Europeans civilisations, with the enlightenment storming across the continent, were the first to fall. Among the last, ironically, would be the African Kingdoms themselves who made unimaginable fortunes from the practice of slavery (as most slaves were not taken by Europeans, but instead by other Africans, who then on-sold their wares to European traders on the Western coasts of the continent). The Kingdom of Benin is probably the most infamous example here. Other civilisational laggards would be found in the Arabic Empires, who dealt with far more African slaves, and for far longer a timeframe, than the Europeans.

Ironically, and devastatingly, there are probably (estimates vary) more slaves alive today than ever before. For all the efforts of those who came before; the evil institution lives on.

Moving on from slavery, we go towards the crowning triumph of the natural law in the modern era – that of the Nuremberg trials. Horrors of an inconceivable scale were inflicted on minority populations (most obviously the Jews of Europe) during the reign of Nazi terror. After the war, what legal framework did the prosecutors rely upon? After all, the actions of the Nazi war machine, the workcamps, the ritual humiliations, and the savagery of institutionalised murder, were all legally permissible (and in fact explicitly commissioned) by the German and her allied governments.

The prosecutors relied on the natural law.

That some things, even if condoned in the black and white of a nation's legal code, cannot, and will *never* be permissible.

These examples show us that while things have changed over time – we have gradually moved towards societies which are generally more pleasant and equitable for us to live within. There are too many examples here for me to mention. Whether it be the Twelve Tables of Rome (the first expansion of rights towards the Plebian class against the Patricians), *Magna Carta* (where

King John's barons *significantly* limited the monarch's ability to rule arbitrarily), The English Bill of Rights and Glorious Revolution (establishing firmly the supremacy of Parliament), and with many more examples besides.

However, I do not wish to give the impression that I view progress as inevitable. It is anything but.

Edmund Burke, writing about the French Revolution and the death of Marie Antoinette,

'I thought that ten thousand swords must have leapt from their scabbards to avenge even a look that threatened her with insult. But that age of chivalry is gone.'

He was right of course, instead of avenging insult – they bound her in painful ropes, paraded her in an open carriage, and cut off her head in front of a crowd baying for blood. I find it not surprising that a revolution baptised in the blood of innocents would fall quickly into the reign of terror. The mob is a dangerous thing.

As Shakespeare wrote of Marc Antony, my favourite line in all of Shakespeare, *"O judgement, thou art fled to Brutish beasts and men have lost their reason!"* Whenever I quote that line, I always capitalise *Brutish* as a proper noun– for obvious reasons. The mob is a dangerous thing.

The law is how we attempt to control these horrid (but all too natural) impulses. To temper our societies when we cannot temper ourselves. Human nature evolved over eons uncounted. We are foolish if we think we can undo it even with all the best teaching in the world. We cannot undo ourselves; we cannot unmake what the forces of nature have made us into. That is the cruel reality of the human condition.

We are frail, we are fallible, we are fallen. We are all these things. Beauty and evil rests within everyone and it is society's job to try and maximise the former and limit the latter. That is, fundamentally, what the law is about. That is what it tries to do.

For the law to do this, however, it requires a constant vigilance. A constant recognition that there is an abyss of eternal blackness not so far from view. A knowledge that things can get very bleak, very quickly.

The immortal law of the universe is that entropy always wins. There can be no victory. Defeat is coming, eventually, and inexorably. We are going to lose the fight at some point. Whether it be our bodies, or our civilisations, or the ideals which we hold most dear – we are all going to lose everything and there is nothing we can do about it.

The strength of a prince in his prime becomes the judgment of a wise king. But wise judgment turns inevitably into the ravings of an old man – slowly losing his senses to senility.

This is a constant thread in the best story ever written, that of the *Lord of the Rings*.

As Galadriel states,

'And together through ages of the world we have fought the long defeat.'[3]

This quote goes to the heart of everything. That we are fighting a losing war. We'll all lose everything eventually. But we have to keep on fighting anyway.

Let's please try and delay the inevitable a little while longer.

---

[3] J R R Tolkien, *The Lord of the Rings* (HarperCollins Publishers, 15th ed, 1995) 348.

I THE SETTLEMENT OF AUSTRALIA

To understand the legal framework of the nation, you must first look at our founding. Australia was formerly a settled colony of the British Empire, basically meaning that once the Union Jack was planted in our soil; English law was imported in its (wholesale) entirety. While this system of government is one of the most stable, and the surrounding adversarial common law dispute resolution process most advantageous; the wholesale importation of English law was not without its own drawbacks unique to Australia. The most obvious of these issues is that simply stating a bunch of land is 'ours' quite clearly pays little heed to the pre-existing native populations. While this has not totally been resolved (and will not be fleshed out within this book) - the current native title system (as outlined by *Mabo*[4] and the later legislation)[5] can effectively be summarised as into a few points:

(a) If you as an indigenous person or group can prove you have a connection (basically meaning observance of traditional customs/law[6] to the land), *and,*

(b) Have had (your ancestors) an ongoing connection to the land since settlement which has not been 'washed away'[7] since settlement; then you may have native title over the land.

If connection to land has also been removed (e.g. via an inconsistent grant) from the legislative or executive – this will also kill native title.

(c) *Note: The native title recognised may not be a mirror image of 'fee simple' ownership (commonly known as just 'owning' the land – i.e. the highest form of land ownership permitted in Australia). Other rights may be protected and others not. For example, the right to hunt/fish on the land may be given without the right of permanent residence; or the right of customary law education may not be given with the right to hunt/fish and so on.

(d) **Note: The law also now recognises that certain native title rights may coexist with traditional rights found within the common law.

---

[4] *Mabo v Queensland (No 2)* (1992) 175 CLR 1.
[5] *Native Title Act 1993* (Cth).
[6] *Mabo v Queensland (No 2)* (1992) 175 CLR 1, 60.
[7] Ibid.

- (e) ***Note: Separate to the above analysis, nothing here may stop a government through individual pieces of legislation from giving land wholesale (or for particular purpose) to an indigenous group directly (as has been done on numerous occasions).
- (f) There are also other laws unique to Indigenous Australians outside of Native Title. Examples of this are myriad – everything from special considerations in the granting of bail (within criminal offences), to increased rights regarding fishing/hunting/gathering of native flora and fauna, and everything in between.

Again, distinct to the native title issue, English law was quickly modified in a few other minor contrivances soon after settlement. This was largely due to the early colony largely consisting of convicts, and (of course), that the laws of England may not be the best way to order a new and fledgling society.

It was often the case, for example, that frontier laws would be a very basic framework which had an underlying English character. In their administration, the 'laws' which governed early settlements may have differed from each other based on the local requirements and the individual matters which fell before the primitive 'courts.'

Decades passed, and the laws of repugnancy were soon enacted – these allowing strong form judicial review (meaning judges could strike down and make void legislation) on statute passed which was inconsistent with the laws of England. Australia was federated (meaning became a bona fide nation in her own right as opposed to simply being a British colony) in 1901. All the states in the current federation chose to enter (with significant trepidation from some – I'm looking at you Western Australia). New Zealand, which was offered a place within the nation, chose to follow her own destiny. Despite our sporting rivalry, I would be remiss if I didn't express some degree of wistful desire for New Zealand to join up eventually. If that were the case, we could claim that the Lord of the Rings (the best movies ever made) were filmed on home soil.

A series of reforms were then passed, post federation, allowing for an ever-higher degree of autonomy - culminating in the final reforms of 1986, in which the High Court was finally designated as the ultimate appeals court of Australia. Also removed was all remaining ability for the United Kingdom to legislate for Australia. This was coupled with the revocation of any repugnancy type constraint on governments which were still somewhat technically present. Interesting to note here is that the courts of the United Kingdom (and those from nations with the same roots – namely the New Zealand and Canadian courts as examples) remain highly persuasive on those of Australia. I can count on my ten fingers and ten toes the number of times Australian precedent has diverged from that of our mother country. While I am (of course) speaking figuratively here, the number remains well within the minority where the substance of the common law (in Australia) differs substantially from that of the law of England and Wales. Continuing with this reasoning; there has been many an occasion in which the development of Australian legal precedent has referenced the case law of England, Canada, and other Commonwealth nations as the guiding principle. It is also not uncommon for Australian jurists to simply import the foreign legal principles wholesale.

The only remaining function of the United Kingdom in Australia is that the de jure head of state remains to be Queen Elizabeth II (and no I don't buy the notion that the Governor-General is our head of state considering they are merely a representative, including as commander-in-chief,[8] for the person wearing the crown). Dad, considering the experience I have gained regarding the difference between de jure and de facto, I would be remiss if I didn't place emphasis on the former. The Crown through the Governor-General may still veto legislation by not giving Royal assent and the Governor-General still maintains the right to dissolve parliament. These latter two are the largest reasons as to why some contend that the Governor-General is the head of state and 'above' the Prime Minister. There are some other rights of the sovereign and her representative remaining, yet these are the big four.

The remaining functions of a traditional head of state (including having the bully pulpit, creating a cabinet, delegating duties to the larger executive, choosing which policy is deserving of priority, and being the 'face of government,' among others) belong to the Prime Minister – the de facto head-of-state. This position also has the ability to effectively appoint the Governor-General, with the Queen essentially 'rubber stamping' whoever is chosen. Nevertheless the final approval must be given by the monarch. Again, there is a fight between de jure and de facto. These arguments aside, considering a series of mistakes I would not have made if I had higher regard to the former, I will certainly do so now. However, the truth, as nearly always, is up for grabs.

Considering the limited role of the monarch in recent decades, a role that is ever decreasing, there is naturally debate regarding whether Australia should sever her ties with the United Kingdom to become a republic. I'm not totally against the idea, nor am I for it for the nearly purely symbolic nature that such a move would entail. Before we answer such a question in the

---

[8] *Commonwealth of Australia Constitution Act 1901* (Cth) s 68.

affirmative; we must first answer for ourselves the more paramount question, at least in my mind, of what the role of the President should be? If the President would have the same role as the current Governor-General; and merely be a puppet of the Prime Minister (say for example as an unelected position put into power by the Prime Minister), then we must ask ourselves what would be the point of such a move? We would be gaining a head-of-state with even less autonomy than the current model, serving as a more ineffective check on the power of the legislature. If, however, the role was elected; crucially with an American style primary (as well) to nominate the candidates from each party – then, and only then, would I *possibly* be supportive of such a move. Having legal requirements that the primaries be conducted on the same day and with these primaries having a specified (short) distance from the date of general election would also be needed (as to avoid the endless marathon of campaigns found in the United States). Again, this is only to have my *theoretical* support. I'm sorry America, I cherish the enlightenment principles that your Declaration of Independence and Constitution espouse, and the Bill of Rights protects – but nearly two years is too long to elect someone for a four-year term.

That's what it would take for me to *possibly* vote away from the incredibly stable and effective constitutional monarchy we have enjoyed. Nevertheless, this is clearly a personal political question. I don't ask that you hold my views; I merely ask you justify whatever opinion you have with reasoned and respectful debate.

As a side note, as the above highlights – I am not totally sold on the idea of a Republic, even in principle. We in Australia have a proud inherited legal tradition – the English legal tradition. Moving away from such a system (one that is the world's most stable) may have consequences we can't even foresee. Monarchies, as a general rule, are far more stable than republics. In the long history of democratic nations falling to tyranny, there have been far more fallen republics than monarchies. Some commentators posit this is due to the position of head of state being occupied by the monarch instead a president, and hence the political realm (and those within) never gain the same levels of adoration and blind devotion that monarchs enjoy. In constitutional monarchies, we view our politicians as tools wielded by the public and for the public interest. When we view them as doing us wrong, we feel the innate ability to tell them that. In republics, with the president as head of state, this is harder to do. The president gains the position as being the person who embodies the nation in flesh, and by the immutable rules of the universe, it is harder to tell that person exactly what we may think of them.

Before we move on, I want to give a brief tangent on the issue of Australia Day. Increasingly, there seems to be pressure to move the date away from what certain portions of the indigenous community hold to be 'invasion day.' I would urge, strongly urge, restraint here. Should Australia Day have been placed on the 26th at first instance? The answer is arguably a resounding no. That being said, it has been the date which countless migrant Australians have become citizens. Australia is now a migrant nation, and this date is symbolic of Australia's fantastic migrant experience – the experience of most Australians (including my own family). Moving this date would possibly be considered an affront to every Australian who has gained citizenship on the day – that somehow the date on which they become citizens of this great country was somehow tainted by sins not committed by themselves. I asked a member of my family this question, and their response was that moving the date (to them), was like saying the story of how they became a citizen didn't matter. I'm not giving my own view one way or the other here (I'll save that for other issues of this book) – lest it simply become a list of my own opinions. I am merely stating that there are two reasonable viewpoints and that we should have this debate soberly and with respect for the other side. Name calling (and particularly calling the contradictory side the worst form of insult – The R word) does nothing but inflame an already hot issue.

I'm never a fan of sweeping issues under the rug. The answer to injustice is sunlight and healing. My father gave his view, and I personally find it a rather reasonable option (although again I'm not necessarily in favour). Recognition of Indigenous Australians' history should also be included on this date. This should include stark references to the previous history of persecution and be committed unreservedly towards the process of healing and righting the wrongs of history. The date would come full circle and be a reminder of the historical injustices and unafraid consensus that it can never be allowed to happen again - without whitewashing history; something that only increases the propensity for the unacceptable to repeat. That's my dad's take at least.

II THE SEPARATION OF POWERS

Australia is a constitutional federation with three arms of government. The justification for having a separation of powers is rather self-evident; for the same reason we don't allow a single body to be judge, jury, and executioner. We also segregate how public authority is wielded, namely by ensuring power is split to various bodies, each with conflicting aims and objectives. Give too much power to a single branch and the liberty of individual citizens is put at risk. We effectively model the Government of the United Kingdom, in most respects, but-for a few main points of conflict - which will be discussed below. Regarding our similarities, the three arms of government within both nations are:

(a) The Legislature: The Parliament has the ability and duty to create laws (statute). While the courts may create the common law through their judgments, statute (with one exception as articulated below), always has the ability to override a court decision. The reasoning here is relatively straight forward – judges are not elected whilst parliamentarians are. Therefore, the 'final say' should rest on the shoulders of whom the majority of public opinion also resides (and whose career belongs in the public's hands). Meaning, they would, in theory, be less inclined to vote for legislation contravening public opinion within their own electorate. Within the English (Westminster) system, parliament is deemed as the most important of the three arms of government; having the largest ability to create public policy and change the legal mechanisms in which societies operate.

(b) The Executive: The executive is responsible for administering the law, not to make it. Within the American political framework there remains a large distinction between the executive and legislature. This is due to the President and various secretaries being absolutely separated from the Congress. The Westminster system of governance however, of which Australia replicates, is unique in this respect; namely that the executive can be separated into a few subcategories with some components *overlapping* with the legislature.

(i) *The Crown:* The most obvious component of the executive – including the Monarch as head of state and their representatives (Governors and Governors-General).

(ii) *Executive Departments:* The various departments have the responsibility of administering the many programs the government offers to citizens (such as the social security framework) and also those ensuring the proper observance law by ordinary citizens (such as the police and other investigatory bodies).

There has been some criticism levied (by more conservative voices) at the recent explosion of this portion of the executive being given quasi legislative powers - in the form of regulations. This is because most current legislation regulating behaviour will effectively allow the executive department to develop their own standards for compliance.

An example of this (and I'm not sure if this is correct; it's merely being used for illustrative purposes) is the parliament passing a statute stating something along the lines of; 'the environmental protection agency shall develop a standard for car emissions, and any automobile contravening their standard shall be deemed ineligible for road use.' Note, that the specific car standards, under such a framework, are not created by the parliament. They are instead given by the parliament to the executive department to develop.

The benefits of having this style of legislation are obvious; namely that the individual members of parliament, on aggregate, are unlikely to have respective expertise in all the areas in which government must regulate – from car emissions, fishing regulations, and many more.

Handing this ability to the executive departments, therefore, effectively allows for those with the relevant expertise to create the regulations.

It also, ideally, enables regulatory flexibility should conditions change. Say the surrounding circumstances around the regulation makes it obsolete or needing modification - instead of the parliament requiring new legislation every single time this occurs, the regulation is simply changed by the department in a more flexible and less resource intensive process.

I'll give a humorous example to illustrate the point. There would be significant opportunity cost (e.g. in time) were the parliament having to pass a new law every time the minimum size of a caught fish was revised (especially considering that parliamentarians likely have no idea what the size of various species of fish are).

It is far easier to give this type of stuff to the departments, who are filled with (in this case) experts, such as biologists, who can accurately tell you what the size of caught fish should be to increase their numbers in our waters.

This applies to the innumerable regulations required within a modern society. If parliament was needed to do every regulation – they would be doing nothing other than updating regulations.

This is the most charitable view of the alphabet soup agencies.

Those more critical of the accelerated move towards an 'administrative state' (myself included) will claim that this increases the impact of decisions made by unelected bodies; effectively consisting of technocrats. The counter to this is that the parliament may still veto (through legislation) the regulations which may be enacted by the executive agencies. Similarly, the regulations must be within the constraints set by the initial statute at first instance. Oversight is good, by its very nature it limits daft decisions by bodies who know their ideas will be scrutinised by somebody else. My primary concern is that legislatures, particularly in within recent years, have become more hesitant to challenge any decision taken by the executive. Similarly, recent legislation (it can be argued) has been creating insufficient boundaries on the types of regulations that can be created by the unelected departments. In order for the executive to function properly, and in the interest of the people, there needs to be a reinvigoration of the scrutinization function of the parliament.

Prime Minister and Cabinet: This is the largest departure from the very clean separation of powers to be found in the American system of government. Namely that the Prime Minister and Cabinet sit within the legislature as members of it. While it is certainly true that when the Prime Minister and members of Cabinet vote on legislation, they are part of the legislature, when exercising their administrative functions (ministers are literally given a 'portfolio' of laws in which they are responsible to administer), they are squarely part of the executive.

(iii) *Tribunals:* While it may initially seem to an external observer that tribunals are essentially courts with a different name; because tribunals are creatures of legislation, and hence the parliament may give (or take away) their powers at any time, they are counted within the executive. This fact is also coupled with the larger factor that they may undertake the very same administrative functions which are constitutionally barred from 'Chapter III Courts' under the *Boilermakers'*[9] principle. As such, these bodies (to reiterate) lie firmly within the executive branch.

(iv) *Note:** Also important is that many executive bodies are given a large degree of independence from their highly politicised colleagues. Examples of this include the commissions which set the minimum working standards (including pay and conditions) within the nation. The original notion for this level of independence is to remove contentious issues (such as industrial relations policies) from the political arena. The benefits for both sides of politics are obvious; through lower opportunity cost (via giving the ability to focus on other issues) and also through having an in-build excuse to follow-through with measures unpopular with the public.

Another benefit is illustrated by the example of the Pharmaceutical Benefits Advisory Committee. This body (and those like it, albeit on different issues) gives independent advice to the Health Minister regarding which drugs should be placed on the Pharmaceutical Benefits Scheme (and hence be heavily subsidised). These expert members of the committee are more highly qualified to make informed decisions regarding which drugs should be subsidised by the taxpayer when compared to the plurality of lawyers, who have never seen the inside of a pharmaceutical lab, sitting within parliament. Again, the question of giving too much power to independent 'experts' versus a democratically elected parliament has proven a difficult balance to strike – particularly within recent years where the

---

[9] *R v Kirby; Ex parte Boilermaker's Society of Australia* (1956) 94 CLR 254.

complexity of most governmental decisions has done nothing but increase.

The Judiciary: The final group within the Australian separation of powers is that of the courts. This body is responsible for interpretation of statute, creating the common law, and ensuring created statute is within the bounds set by the constitution.

This is the first departure of the Australian system versus the English. That is, courts in Australia maintain the ability to strike down legislation which is non-compliant with the constitution - in 'strong form' judicial review. This is unavailable to the pure model of parliamentary sovereignty found in the United Kingdom. American readers will note that this is clearly a replication of the United States framework; whereby the courts also have the final say in whether legislation is compliant with the founding document.

This system ensures that the parliament cannot remove individual rights and liberties of ordinary citizens on a whim or enforce the possibly detrimental wishes of the ruling majority onto a weaker minority. Such an ability is crucial for the functioning of a free state, over the long term, through the limiting of a 'chipping away' of rights by the legislature (preventing a removal of the specified rights given by the constitution). An example of this can be given in privacy rights set against those of political speech. The latter being (impliedly) protected by the constitution and the former not. This creates the situation in which privacy expectations have been argued, by civil liberties groups for example, to have been continuously removed by successive governments. This is as opposed to political speech - which is less able to have the same legislative erosion imposed upon it.

It is for this reason I argue strongly for a Bill of Rights – something which would expand the current scant protections offered by the constitution. This would further limit the governmental ability to encroach upon that enlightenment ideal of individual liberty. A further explanation of the current rights protection framework shall be discussed in further sections of the book.

As mentioned, there are a few differences between the Australian and English model. The first, being the ability for strong-form judicial review, is spoken about above. The other main difference is that Australia is a constitutional federation – meaning that the states have intrinsic powers to legislate in areas in which the federal government may not. Should the federal government attempt to legislate in areas left for the states, such as intra-state trade (subject to few exceptions), this legislation will be deemed invalid. The same can be true in the other direction, should the state attempt to legislate in a matter reserved for the Commonwealth, this will also be equally void. In the areas in which state and federal governments have the ability to legislate, and the statutes conflict – to the extent of the conflict, the legislation of the state government will be deemed subordinate to the federal and hence the federal legislation prevails.[10]

Just be careful about your phrasing here – please try to refrain from using the word 'reserved' when referring to state powers. The case of *Engineers*[11] made it very clear that the notion of 'reserved' state powers was obsolete. It is more helpful to look at the restrictions as limits on federal power (with state power filling in the gaps) as opposed to the states limiting the Commonwealth.

---

[10] *Commonwealth of Australia Constitution Act 1901* (Cth) s 109.
[11] *Amalgamated Society of Engineers v Adelaide Steamship Co Ltd* (1920) 28 CLR 129.

III Rights Protection In Australia

A *Constitutional Protection*

As already mentioned above, there are certain (albeit a small selection) of rights which enjoy constitutional protection. Just note that the court, since federation, has often interpreted these express rights as lessor than one might spontaneously imagine. The paradigm exception to this 'reading down' of constitutional protections by the court is the requirement that citizens of one state need to be treated without discrimination by other states. This particular right was, ironically, litigated and affirmed in the context of a lawyer of one state wanting to be a lawyer in another.[12]

1 *Trial by Jury*[13]

This right exists in federal indictable offences. This is perhaps the most famous right in which the court has impliedly removed protection from a rather express term. The court has been unwilling to grant this aegis to all serious criminal trials at a federal level. The parliament may therefore pick and choose which crimes are to be tried by the above formal process and hence may simply skirt around the wording of the section.

2 *Freedom of and from Religion*[14]

In a similar manner to the above protection being minimal due to the court's interpretation of the section – the same can be said here. Short of the government actually establishing a religious test for various postings, or in the building and promoting of an official religion, there seems to be ample scope for an overlaying of church and state. Even something akin to the government mandating the end of a religious branch during wartime and seizing their

---

[12] *Commonwealth of Australia Constitution Act 1901* (Cth) s 117.
[13] Ibid s 80.
[14] Ibid s 116.

respective property has been deemed to be within the governmental prerogative;[15] a toothless tiger if there ever was one.

3 Voting Rights in Federal Elections[16]

Basically, if you were of the age to vote in a state election at the time when the constitution entered into force; you could vote in federal elections. While the states had slightly different definitions for who was given suffrage – generally speaking those over 21 years of age were deemed by the court as eligible to vote.[17]

There have been a whole host of cases since Federation delineating the right to vote and the ability for the parliament to take away this right. Essentially, the rule, as developed by the High Court, is that the parliament may skirt around the edges of this right in some limited circumstances. If, however, the fundamental character of Australia's universal franchise is damaged by some legislation – the court will intervene and deem the offending law invalid.

4 Just Terms[18]

Perhaps the most famous constitutional right is that the Commonwealth may only acquire property on just terms. What 'just' means is rather clearly the crucial issue for determination. The court has (basically) defined it with reference to an objective standard of fairness (i.e. could the process be reasonably said to be fair). The entire *Durham*[19] judgment provides perhaps the most detailed explanation of which. If you're in the mood to be entertained, the Australian movie 'The Castle,' has its plot revolve around this right. Tell him he's dreaming.

---

[15] *Adelaide Company of Jehovah's Witnesses Incorporated v Commonwealth* (1943) 67 CLR 116.
[16] *Commonwealth of Australia Constitution Act 1901* (Cth) ss 7, 24, 41.
[17] *King v Jones* (1972) 128 CLR 221 (Stephen J).
[18] *Commonwealth of Australia Constitution Act 1901* (Cth) s 51 (xxxi).
[19] *Durham Holdings Pty Ltd v New South Wales* (2001) 205 CLR 399.

5 *Freedom of Speech*

Freedom of political communication has been impliedly supported by the court (first in *Lange*[20] then with a more detailed test in *McCloy)*[21] to be protected by the constitution. Without becoming too technical, the current state of the law is effectively whether the burdens on speech become too onerous (suggesting there need be a burden) for the law's *legitimate* objective to be met. Basically, there is a balancing act between the requirement of freedom of speech, compared to the mending of whatever ill the law was designed to fix. Should the balance be met, and the legislation be congruent with the overall functioning of Australia's democratic system of government, then the law will likely stand.

6 *Others*

There are some other parts in the constitution which may be interpreted as citizens' rights but are not directly referred to as such. The first of which being the right of citizens to seek court review of executive government decisions for jurisdictional error. This rights exists regardless of statutory limitations[22] (a portion of administrative law which will be given its own stand-alone section of the book). The right of free interstate commerce[23] may also be described as a crucial freedom by the business community.

B *Statutory Interpretation*

The common law requires that a statute be interpreted in a manner consistent with human rights and hence any attempted removal of these rights by the parliament need be expressly stated. This is known as the 'principle of legality.' The logic here is relatively straight forward; parliamentarians are elected by their constituents and hence they would be less likely to revoke their electors' rights if they must make any attempt to do so immediately obvious. Likewise, the argument holds that should the constituency support the removal of certain rights in an

---

[20] *Lange v Australian Broadcasting Corporation* (1997) 189 CLR 520.
[21] *McCloy v New South Wales* (2015) 257 CLR 178.
[22] *Kirk v Industrial Court of New South Wales* (2010) 239 CLR 531.
[23] *Commonwealth of Australia Constitution Act 1901* (Cth) s 92.

express manner; in a Westminster democracy this should equally be supported. The issue with this reasoning is that, as often is the case, constituents are not politically minded enough to keep a constant watch over the actions of the legislature. Nor are the rights of the minority (over the majority) sufficiently protected. In addition to these criticisms, the parliament may slowly 'chip away' at rights piecemeal, and thereby, over the long term – leave the citizenry unprotected. This is similar to the analogy of the live frog being placed into cold water - not noticing the increase in temperature until it is simply too late to do anything about it.

C *Legislative Processes*

The Commonwealth Parliament, in the drafting process of legislation, has the Bill go through what is effectively a committee type procedure to determine whether the law is compatible with human rights, and if not, what rights are impacted. This process naturally has no ability to change the soon 'to be legislation' above the possibility of a deterrence. In Victoria and the ACT (where there are statutory Bills of Rights), the courts in these states are empowered to release statements (post legislation being passed) which highlight again if the law is compatible with the human rights regime and what rights are affected. Again, above the increased deterrence to the government, the courts cannot engage in strong-form judicial review to strike down such laws and hence the 'frog' and 'minority' problems above still stand.

The Australian Human Rights Commission is another vocal body which makes a big fuss every time the government does something annoying. But, as the alleged human rights abuses in the realm of refugees within recent decades has shown, the organisation has little impact upon government decision making (above the possible effect on public opinion which may change election outcomes).

Going on a tangent, the issue of refugees in Australia is one of the areas in which I have found large frustration. It seems both sides of the debate have not realised (or do not admit) there is no silver bullet to be found in this area. As Thomas Sowell so eloquently stated, 'there are no solutions – there are only trade-offs.'

Australia is not going to be overrun with too many refugees if asylum seekers by boat are not kept in long term detention. The issue with allowing this (and not providing a disincentive), however, is that people drown in the ocean on the journey to Australian shores. Australia is an island with relatively rough waters around our beaches, and no policy will change this fact. As such, if people are not disincentivized to come by boat – some will (inevitably) drown in the water. Children, who have no way (children are deemed to not have this capacity) of actually consenting to their parents' decision to come by boat, still face the cold reality that they may fall victim to rough seas all the same and drown. Even one child dying on this journey is too many, although the numbers of this have been far higher in recent years. People's hearts may be in the right place here, but again, there is no silver bullet. My proposed solution would be to maintain the current disincentive regime (so that kids don't drown in the water thanks to their parents' decisions) - albeit with less prison-esque conditions. Similarly, there should be free reign for journalists, doctors, educators, and anyone else to shine a light and make complaints about conditions within detention camps.

To compensate for this, the numbers of refugees accepted from other means (such as United Nations' camps) should be increased as an admittedly imperfect offset. Even if you don't happen to agree with this position, I think we can all agree that this issue is too often dealt with as merely a mechanism to score political points and 'rally the base' on one side or another. If we have any dignity at all, this needs to stop.

D *Common Law*

Tort law has been argued to be a sufficient protector of human rights in Australia by those who agree with the Westminster notion of parliamentary supremacy. Torts against assault, false imprisonment, negligence, defamation, trespass, conversion, and others are supported as adequate protections of person and property.

The counter to this is that because these 'rights' are protected within the common law, there is nothing stopping the legislature from simply removing them. As such, this may not provide adequate protection against the government itself – whom civil libertarians (such as myself) deem as the primary adversary to individual freedom over the long term.

Please also note that most of the above torts will be dealt with within their own sections, later in this book.

E *Privacy Protection*

In an era of increasing communication via the internet, privacy has become a paramount concern for civil libertarians. What is interesting, however, is that the Australian constitution does not protect this right at all; nor does the common law (e.g. through a tort of privacy - yet) generally protect individuals in most circumstances. The following will detail the current privacy protection regime.

1 *A Whole Bunch of Statutes*

There are numerous pieces of legislation littered around the legal framework of Australia detailing the requirement of privacy in certain, generally professional-client type, instances. Health workers, lawyers, specific government bureaucrats, and other like professions each have their own statutory requirements that information about the clients or patients they serve remains confidential. As with all things, there are some exceptions to these rules. Exceptions are varied and are usually specific to the profession in question and the particular circumstances of the matter. An example from my own profession, as a doctor, is that certain health information may be necessary to divulge - such as the information pertaining to sexual (or other) abuse of minors/children.

2 *A Tort of Privacy*

The funniest case I've ever read in law school has got to be *Victoria*.[24] Basically there was this racetrack, and unsurprisingly, races were conducted here for money (people buy tickets to see the race). Some guy, 'Taylor,' thought it would be a great idea to allow the building of this platform in his neighbouring house to physically look into the racecourse (to see the outcome of the races). Google the platform he used, there is a photo online and trust me you'll want to see it.

---

[24] *Victoria Park Racing and Recreation Grounds Co Ltd v Taylor* (1937) 58 CLR 479.

The information on the races and their outcomes was then given to a radio station and people would listen in - instead of going to the race. The company sued for their loss (as fewer people were buying tickets now that they could listen to the outcome).

The remainder of the case goes on to say that there is no tort of privacy recognised in Australian law. The obvious solution to the racecourse owners were that the company should therefore just build a bigger fence to keep away prying eyes. This precedent hasn't overly changed since the early 20th century. The 21st century case of *Lenah Game*[25] pretty much says the same thing, albeit leaving the door slightly ajar (in typical High Court fashion) to the recognition of this tort in the future. Similarly, there have been more recent rumblings of the tort being recognised. Watch this space.

3 *Breach of Confidence*

So now we move from the common law torts to the equitable jurisdiction. Before I begin going through the rules here, there needs to be a discussion of the difference between equity and the common law.

Nowadays, there is not as big a distinction between the two jurisdictions. Previously, a litigant would need to literally go to a different court (or Chancellor) to seek a remedy here. Post the Judicature Acts of the 1870's, however, this distinction was effectively removed and now the doctrines of equity and those found within the common law can be utilised within the same court. One must be careful however to not simply equate the two areas of law; they remain very different with their own peculiar rules. Just for reference, equity, on aggregate, was developed to blunt the cold and harsh edge of the common law - and as its name suggests. It primarily deals with issues of fundamental fairness and in areas of asymmetric (to the point of unfairness) knowledge/expertise between the parties of a case. Examples of equitable jurisdiction include estoppel, trusts, fiduciary relationships, and breaches of confidence.

Moving to the topic at hand, breaches of confidence can traditionally be summarised in the English (which although is not technically binding on Australian courts – remains highly persuasive) law case which I personally find the most illustrative. The law here can be

---

[25] *Australian Broadcasting Corporation v Lenah Game Meats Pty Ltd* (2002) 208 CLR 199.

summarised into three parts (some textbooks say four or five parts – but I've amalgamated what I can into the simplest crux of the rules):[26]

(i) *Nature/Content/Type of the Information – Information is sufficiently confidential:* The information breached must effectively be private enough to be deserving of protection. The Australian case of *Lenah Game*[27] provides a pretty detailed explanation of what this actually entails through the rather apt description of a 'man in his underwear'[28] being sufficiently private to pass the first threshold. Back in law school one of my mates was rather taken aback by this quote (I've gotten their permission to give this story so long as I don't disclose personal details – lest I myself be liable for a breach!).

Back to the story, when doing readings for this particular class (we did them together) we came upon this phrase from *Lenah*. Upon sight of the phrase 'underwear' they immediately told me how they were really worried about photos of themselves in a similar situation 'getting out.' The photos were not criminal in any way, being not particularly revealing (baggy superhero themed boxer shorts to be precise; no worse than any guy at the beach in swimwear). Nonetheless, they were embarrassing, and my mate later confided in me how they may have had a little 'freak out' over the incident following that class!

Just note now that while breaches of confidence are illegal (in the same way breaching a contract is illegal – i.e. being contrary to law) they are not criminal in any way, shape, or form.

(ii) *How Content/Information was Given – Obligations of Confidentiality:* The information must have been given in a manner which necessarily obligates the individual to retain confidence of said content. So, for example, if I pick up a printed email on the side of the road that has confidential stuff therein – it would be unlikely that the obligation would apply to me as the mere 'finder' of such material.

---

[26] *Coco v A N Clark (Engineers) Ltd* [1969] RPC 41 (Megarry J).
[27] *Australian Broadcasting Corporation v Lenah Game Meats Pty Ltd* (2002) 208 CLR 199.
[28] Ibid (Gleeson CJ).

The outcome would likely be very different if I had specifically requested that the same confidential email was sent to me directly and especially if I had made some undertakings that I would keep it a secret.

(iii) *Use of Information:* Clearly there is no breach of confidence if the discloser was given the 'go ahead' from the person to whom the information belongs. The disclosure must be unauthorised. Necessarily, therefore, there must be a disclosure from the person to whom one gave confidential information to the wider world or some other unauthorised person.

I only bring this second point up because my mate had made a mistake on this particular point. He had insisted that the recipient merely 'keeping hold' of the photos post the consent being withdrawn was enough to be a breach of confidence. This is not the case, consent is a 'once-and-for-all' type mechanism here (i.e. once consent is given to the other party - shown by you giving them the photos/information/whatever is private) then they retain said consent. It only becomes a breach of confidence if they then show someone else the confidential material without your consent being given.

4 *Bill of Rights*

Now if we really wanted to ensure that the government couldn't pass a law stating that intelligence gathering agencies could simply peruse through your personal emails, or tap your phone, or look through your house (all without a warrant) we would codify such a regime in the constitution. Post the same sex marriage vote; I have heard some rumblings that this may be supported by both sides of politics (the right wanting to protect religious freedoms for example). Naturally, time will tell if this bears any fruit. I would be remiss if I didn't point out that such rumblings have been felt before on a few occasions – and have never amounted to much.

As an addition from 2022, the last few years (since I wrote this book) have been disastrous for freedoms within the Western World. Privacy, freedom of speech, freedom of assembly, the rights of a fair trial (such as the presumption of innocence and the right to test the evidence brought by your accuser with a *strong* cross-examination) have all been assaulted in a way I wouldn't have thought possible even a few years ago. If ever there was a time to enshrine the rights which our forefathers have bled for - it is now.

IV Administrative Law

One tenant of any society which maintains a separation of powers is that ordinary citizens who are subject to executive mandates can challenge these decisions through another arm of government – namely through the judiciary. The process of appealing a decision of the executive government is aptly named administrative law (the law surrounding those who administer/enforce it).

An example of an administrative law matter is a citizen applying for social security type benefits and getting rejected by the department – they then wish to appeal the decision. The rules surrounding the rejection, what avenues of appeal are available, and the conduct of such appeals are the core of administrative law. The amount of administrative law matters dealt with by the courts has exploded in the post war era (in correspondence with the increase in size and scope of the executive arm of government). The administrative law process is complex, with many moving parts, and with changes being conducted perpetually after each election. The regime is effectively the following:

A *Non Tribunal/Court*

Generally, the first step in reviewing any decision is forcing the relevant department to take another shot at making it. This is called internal review and effectively is a *de novo* appeal to the same department (who made the original decision). Perhaps a more senior member of the department or simply another agent at the same level makes the decision again. Naturally, this form of review has been criticised on the grounds of bias towards collegiality and also does nothing to stop the same, perhaps 'agency level,' faulty processes being used twice.

These problems increase the propensity for the decision (possibly the objectively incorrect one) to remain unchanged. These problems aside, this is obviously (through not requiring external resources) the most efficient manner in challenging a decision, and as such, may be a legal requirement (depending on what is being challenged) before any challenger to a decision is permitted to take it further.

Another avenue which is available to the aggrieved citizen within Australia is to take the matter to their local member of Parliament. Unlike most of Western Europe (with proportional representation) the Australian parliamentary system still runs on the local member – with elections being conducted for an individual to represent a particular electorate. As such, one of the most common methods to communicate problems within the system is for the citizen to tell their local representative of whatever issue they are having. Ideally, this local member then deals with the issue on their behalf – either speaking directly with the high-ranking officials within the department or in attempting to steer the legislature to directly cure the ill through statute.

The ombudsman is another body with extensive investigatory powers which may provide a remedy, through negotiation (the office has little coercive power), with the executive department. The ombudsman may also conduct inquiries/investigations into the processes of various departments without a citizen complaint. They may then make recommendations to the department or to the legislature to change the processes/policy used, or in the moulding of the surrounding statutory framework. Also, important to note, is that complaints are not limited towards a merits type issue (i.e. did the department/decision maker make the 'right' call) regarding the decision of the executive. That is, complaints may also be made towards maladministration on their part. Examples of this include delays, rudeness, and general unprofessionalism.

Some have suggested the office should be granted expanded coercive powers to mould departmental policy; as currently any change rests solely on either convincing the department to fix its own issues, or in doing the same to the legislature to change the law. I personally don't reside under that particular tent. Such a move (in my mind) would be enabling a single arm of the executive (the ombudsman) to have the power to change the policy of departments by themselves. Considering the ideally specialised expertise of the department and comparing it to the generalist knowledge of the ombudsman – giving the ombudsman such coercive powers may actually serve to *increase* maladministration over the long term.

B *Tribunal*

The next most onerous step is an appeal to an Administrative Tribunal – a body of experts conducting an inquisitorial (not adversarial like a traditional court) inquiry into the merits of such a decision. 'Merits review' meaning the objective and factual correctness of a decision – i.e. did the agency make the right call in granting/not granting whatever they did/did not grant.

The advantages of this are obvious for an applicant – a cheaper body (ideally not needing legal representation) which is entitled to (and obligated to) discern whether the objectively correct decision was made at first instance. The tribunal can also insert its own judgment where it feels necessary.

This is likely more beneficial to the applicant, versus a court, due to the courts generally being unable to conduct merits inquiry (and may also not generally substitute their own judgments). I say generally here because the courts (as I will discuss below) can decide a decision was unreasonable (effectively a merits inquiry) in certain circumstances.

I'll make a few extra points about the tribunals. Some commentators *really* don't like them. While legal representation is *ideally* not necessary, a substantial portion of those who receive an adverse decision from a department seek legal advice anyway (as is their right) before appealing to the tribunal. Similarly, those who get an adverse decision at the tribunal level are still usually entitled to appeal to the courts. As such, some commentators argue that while the tribunals are good, *in principle,* they may simply provide an extra barrier (in both cost and time) to an individual who is attempting to appeal an adverse executive decision.

As a side note, the Australian federal election of 2022 has just been had. The coalition (our term for the union of the Liberal and Nationals parties) – has just lost government. Labor, which has just formed a government, has promised to scrutinise the 'Administrative Appeals Tribunal.' As such, the future and makeup of administrative tribunals in Australia is very much a 'watch this space,' at the moment.

C *Judicial Review*

The final stage in administrative review is to the courts. Courts, as opposed to tribunals, are engaged in an adversarial inquiry into the legality (as opposed to the merits) of a decision.

Effectively, the court does not mind if the departmental decision was not (objectively) the best to be made. The courts do care, however, that the decision was legally open to them and that the surrounding process was conducted properly. There is one exception to this general rule, which shall be spoken about in the following section under the 'grounds of review.' Just note now that the ability to seek review for jurisdictional error (essentially a finding that the executive department was acting beyond its authority in the making of a decision) is protected by the separation of powers, within the constitution, at both a state and federal level.[29] What is equally interesting to note, is that it is the court which decides what constitutes a jurisdictional error, and hence, the court finds itself in a position in which they create for themselves the ability to conduct a review into government (executive government) decisions. This is an important ability for the court to maintain – mainly because legislation could otherwise be written to effectively exclude the executive from review; in which case the executive departments (in such cases) could make whatever decisions they so wished and would be above reproach.

Just note that private bodies exercising a public function are generally not subject to judicial review in Australia. This is best illustrated in the case of *NEAT*;[30] essentially the private body here was permitted to promote its own private interests when exercising the public function. Primarily because of this, the ability for judicial review of decisions made by this private body was judged to be non-existent. This decision has been criticised largely on the basis that it may enable the government to remove certain decisions from review simply by giving the decision-making process to a private body. In an era of government increasingly privately contracting services; such a decision will produce a large degree of downward pressure on the ability for individual citizens to seek review of decisions which have administrative type impacts.

Since *NEAT* there have been a few cases which have dealt with the same issue again. Lower courts, in particular, have been careful to 'push the boundaries' of the *NEAT* precedent and attempt to allow for judicial review of private decisions if they have an administrative law flavour. Again, watch this space.

---

[29] *Kirk v Industrial Court of New South Wales* (2010) 239 CLR 531.
[30] *Neat Domestic Training Pty Ltd v AWB Ltd* (2003) 216 CLR 277.

1 Remedies

(a) *Mandamus:* Basically, this is a court order that forces a *public body* to perform a *public duty*. As the above sentence pretty much outlines – the body on which *mandamus* is given must be a public body (not private organisations) and must be acting in their public capacity (as opposed to contractual matters as an example). Just note that mandamus is one of the remedies explicitly protected by the constitution.[31] The remedy does not force the decision to be made in the applicants favour, merely that it be made a second time.

(b) *Prohibition:* As the name suggests, this is an order to block the executive from doing something (generally stopping it making an order which would be made with jurisdictional error). This remedy is also protected by the constitution.[32]

(c) *Injunction:* This remedy is similar to prohibition in the sense that an injunction is also an order stopping the executive from action. Injunctions, however, are more directed at stopping the executive from acting on an already made order, rather than ending the decision-making process itself. This remedy is therefore more a, 'stop doing something,' type order, as opposed to prohibition being more akin to a, 'don't do something,' type order.

(d) *Certiorari:* Quashes (removes legal force – i.e. makes meaningless) an already made decision of the executive. Just note that this remedy is not listed in the constitution. Likewise, this order is auxiliary in the federal jurisdiction, meaning it must be used in conjunction with one of the above orders. However, his is not true for the state jurisdiction. This distinction aside, the order, both at a federal and state level, is generally used with mandamus – with *certiorari* killing the existing order and *mandamus* forcing the decision to be made again.

(e) *Declaration:* This is perhaps the most peculiar remedy; in that it is simply a statement by the court regarding whether the action of the executive was legal or not. The remedy does not change the legal position of the parties, nor does it force/prevent any actions

---

[31] *Commonwealth of Australia Constitution Act 1901* (Cth) s 75(v).
[32] Ibid.

from occurring. Thankfully, our governments are usually quick to remedy the illegality (of whatever they were doing unlawfully) simply because government officials within Australia (and the Western World more broadly) respect the rule of law. This high level of respect for the separation of powers is necessary for the functioning of the Westminster system of government.

Going on a quick tangent, denigrators of our current system often point to the legislature becoming less of a 'check' on executive government power than in previous eras. Parliament, the argument follows, has been claimed to be more of a mere rubber stamp for cabinet decisions than in previous epochs. Continued vigilance is therefore required by the general public to not stand for (and vote for) any parliament that does not adequately hold the executive to account.

2 *Grounds of Review*

While the following list is somewhat extensive and covers a good portion of the judicial review landscape, it is by no means conclusive.

(a) *Application of Policy:* Each decision of the executive needs to be made on its own facts and in line with the statutory underpinnings on which the government is given their authority. As often is the case, various departments mould policy towards their actions as to achieve uniformity in decision making. This is not particularly controversial nor is it problematic. Notwithstanding the above commentary – should the executive department make the decision *simply* on the basis of policy, in lieu of other relevant factors (and the legislation does not make any mention of allowing policy to the exclusion of other matters; or allowing the department to use whatever it deems relevant with full autonomy) then the authority given to this particular part of the executive has not been properly exercised and hence a court will likely deem the decision void.[33]

Just note there is a distinction between a court deciding the decision was invalid (i.e. suffering from jurisdiction error) and merely being unlawful (incorrect in some, smaller way). The former leading to the decision being deemed 'void from the start' (i.e. a

---

[33] *Green v Daniels* (1977) 13 ALR 1, 8.

decision was legally never made) and the latter having a decision being made incorrectly in some fashion. This may seem a distinction without a difference to an observer - but the truth couldn't be further from that simplistic conclusion. In the former category, every subsequent decision is also devoid of legal force (from declaration) as opposed to not being so in the latter scenario. There are further differences as well; but for the moment we'll leave it here.

(b) *Bias:* The reasoning for including bias in the possible grounds of review is self-evident; namely that there needs to be a high degree of public confidence and trust in the decisions of public departments, upon which, so much of society depends. Any possibility that decisions are being made for self-serving reasons would undermine public confidence in government processes and society more generally. There are two categories of bias that may be reviewed:

(i) *Actual Bias:* Exactly what it says on the tin – decisions *actually* made with an in-built bias on the part of the decision maker. Basically that the decision maker's mind is closed to the alternative to his/her point of view.[34] Because this is an inquiry into the subjective, proving this is damn well hard to do. Generally, proof of a financial conflict is the best bet to secure a successful (from the applicant's perspective) review. But-for obvious financial benefit to the decision maker in deciding either way, with emails stating, 'I'm deciding for these dodgy reasons,' proving (subjective) actual bias is really quite unlikely.

(ii) *Apprehended Bias:* This category is primarily based off the notion that decisions should also appear safe from bias (for the reasons listed above) in conjunction with *actually* being so. Basically, the test is objective, being whether a reasonable ~~man~~ person (I've done this on purpose, older legal decisions usually have the phrase 'reasonable man' – newer decisions, for politically correct reasons, have the phrase 'reasonable person' instead) would reasonably deem the decision maker as not bringing full impartiality to the decision.

---

[34] *Minister for Immigration and Multicultural Affairs v Jia* (2001) 205 CLR 507.

My favourite case in administrative law illustrates this well. In *Creasy*[35] a decision was being made by the Minister. Two lower rank dudes who were involved in the overall process, in its early stages, had a financial interest in the decision. The applicant, obviously wanting the decision to go their way, claimed this showed bias, as the two dudes may have influenced the Minister's later determination. The court dashed the applicant's hopes. I will always remember my comments at law school on this matter, when asked by the lecturer what the court's reasoning was; I in all my wisdom said something to the effect of, 'the court basically said these roosters weren't important enough.' I know you're not meant to laugh at your own jokes, but every time I think of my comments, I'm guilty as sin on that score. Moving away from my tangent, clearly the outcome (probably) would have been different if the Minister's own financial interests were conflicted with that of the applicants. Similarly, if the two roosters were of higher rank within the department, a claim of bias may have been successful.

(c) *Fair Hearing:* This is arguably the most expanded upon 'ground of review.' Effectively this ensures that decisions contrary to an applicant's interests are made with the applicant having the right to respond to information that is negative to their claim. I'll give a silly but illustrative example. You are a miner hoping to get a mining licence to dig in a particular area. You apply to the relevant department to gain your licence. In this process, an anonymous letter comes to the department saying that you shouldn't be permitted to mine the area because the last time you ran such an operation you were a one man pollution/waste dumping machine. The department doesn't tell you about the letter, it then takes it into paramount consideration, and then denies you the license. Naturally, you'd be pretty salty that you didn't get a chance to respond to such allegations, be they true or not. This ground ensures that the above does not occur and that you have the right to respond to negative allegations. On a side note, in some older cases you'll see the words 'natural justice,' if you see them – they mean fair hearing.

Similarly, while some newer cases suggest the 'threshold' issue is no longer an accurate statement of the law; considering the lack of complete revocation, we should still consider it. Basically, the leading judgment here, has the fair hearing rule apply to all

---

[35] *Hot Holdings Pty Ltd v Creasy* (2002) 210 CLR 438.

decisions having the ability (and meeting the threshold) to directly impact an applicant's rights or interests. [36] So, for example, a decision whether to grant you a mining license has it applying - this is against something more amorphous and less impactful on you (where the protections may not apply).

(d) *Unreasonableness:* This is my favourite ground of review – by far. Earlier I mentioned that judicial review is limited to a legal inquiry - i.e. it is not permitted to delve into a merits inquiry but must stick to the legality (or not) of the decision making process. This ground of review is arguably the exception to this rule. Unreasonableness has two definitions; the traditional definition, and the newer. The traditional was effectively that a decision is so unreasonable (daft) that no sensible decision maker (who has thought about the problem) could have come to that conclusion.[37] This ground takes its name after the leading case, if you hear anyone refer to the '*Wednesbury*' ground – they are referring to this.

As is pretty plain to see, there is a large degree of circular reasoning here – i.e. something is unreasonable if it is unreasonable. Some have found this an issue; it is effectively unreasonable if the judge at the time deems it so. Because of this problem, newer judgments on the issue refer to a 'better' test here – being effectively whether the decision was 'evident and intelligible.'[38] This newer definition lacks the circular reasoning problem of the older definition and may provide more clarity to the bench (and bar) on this issue. Further refinement in the court of appeal has said that if 'reasonable minds may disagree on whether the decision was reasonable; then it is not unreasonable.'[39] This again adds a higher degree of uniformity on this score.

(e) *More Grounds:* Please be aware there are further grounds of review. These include jurisdictional error (that is, whether the executive decision maker even had the legal ability to make the decision in the first place) – among others.

---

[36] *Kioa v West* (1985) 159 CLR 550, 584 (Mason J).
[37] *Associated Provincial Picture Houses Ltd v Wednesbury Corporation* [1948] 1 KB 223, 229.
[38] *Minister for Immigration and Citizenship v Li* (2013) 249 CLR 332 [76].
[39] *Murrumbidgee Groundwater Preservation Association Inc v Minister for Natural Resources* [2005] NSWCA 10 [152].

3 Standing

Before one is entitled to apply for judicial review, you must first satisfy the standing threshold. Just note the following analysis is contingent upon the legislation not expressly allowing universal standing (called 'open standing') which enables anyone to challenge an executive decision. The courts have illustrated three instances whereby standing will be granted.

(a) *Special Interest:* The leading case of *Australian Conservation Foundation*[40] articulates that an applicant with a 'special interest' in the decision will be granted standing. This special interest is described as being 'higher than an emotional/intellectual concern or the winning of a contest.'[41] Likewise, the applicant need have a higher interest than that of an ordinary member of the public.[42] The case of *Tasmanian*[43] lists a whole bunch of indicia which may serve to illustrate what a special standing may entail – among these being: the organisation being publically funded, representing a large portion of expert opinion, and having long term commitment to the contextual issue being litigated. The size of the organisation *may* also be relevant.

(b) *Direct Interest:* A direct interest can be categorised as a peculiar form of special interest – basically that an individual's rights/interests (such as financial matters) are directly impacted by the executive decision. The cases suggest that any 'direct interest' (particularly financial matters) evidences strongly a special interest being present[44] (as an applicant who may suffer financial loss from any decision is likely categorised as having the decision causing a larger impact on themselves when compared to the wider public).[45]

(c) *Attorney General:* The Attorney is effectively the chief law enforcement officer of the jurisdiction, and thereby in the Westminster tradition, has universal standing in the enforcement and administration of public-law.[46] In previous decades, the Attorney was seen as distinct from ordinary members of Cabinet, effectively given free rein to support

---

[40] *Australian Conservation Foundation Incorporated v Commonwealth* (1979) 146 CLR 493.
[41] Ibid [20].
[42] *Onus v Alcoa of Australia Ltd* (1981) 149 CLR 27 [5].
[43] *Tasmanian Conservation Trust Inc v Minister for Resources* (1995) 55 FCR 516 (Sackville J).
[44] *Bateman's Bay Local Aboriginal Land Council v Aboriginal Community Benefit Fund Pty Ltd* (1998) 194 CLR 247.
[45] *Onus v Alcoa of Australia Ltd* (1981) 149 CLR 27 [9]-[12].
[46] Ibid.

the judiciary despite the possibility of court judgments going against the government of which they are a member. Increasingly however, in more recent years, this office holder has become ever more political - to the point of alleged partisanship in some cases. Attorneys General have therefore been decreasing in propensity to depart from government policy within the public arena.

4 *Justiciability*

The final (or perhaps the first) issue for discussion is whether the matter attempted to be litigated can be reviewed by the judiciary at all. Whether something is justiciable or not is a matter of the nature and subject matter of the case. Matters of relating to executive decisions made under/via legislative power are generally regarded as justiciable.

This is contrasted with 'polycentric' decisions - decisions with many and/or conflicting components/aspirations. These more 'public policy' type determinations are typically dealt with within the realm of the political process, and as such, are usually exempt from judicial review. Similarly, decisions made by political operatives with a high degree of accountability, such as through elections, are also less likely to attract the ability for judicial review. I remember distinctly an example given to my administrative law class by our charismatic lecturer. He gave an example (a hypothetical) of an individual who was declined a licence to build an extension on his house by the department of environment – something which would almost certainly be available for review. He contrasted this with executive decisions regarding foreign policy;[47] which is the paradigm circumstance of a matter excluded from judicial oversight. The former being a case in which the court has a high degree of expertise (essentially being a matter of statutory interpretation) versus the latter in which the courts are fundamentally unequipped to grapple with and have little relevant experience.

---

[47] See, eg, *R (Abbasi) v Secretary of State for Foreign and Commonwealth Affairs, Ex parte Abbasi* [2003] UKHRR 76 CA. As a side note, I reference this case because a heated debate was had by my friend group on the correctness (or not) of the decision. The case is also a good read to see just how careful the courts are in not overstepping into the political realm.

V Criminal Laws

Here is where Australia's legal framework becomes more fragmented. Most criminal legislation is left as a matter for the states, and hence, while the 'vibes' of criminal law are pretty much universal between the states - some differences remain. The following will effectively be a list of the most well-known crimes within Australia from the viewpoint of New South Wales (my home state).

Just note there are also a few points of extreme importance to be mentioned before delving into the laws themselves.

A *What Does Criminal Law Defend Against?*

Criminal law protects against a breach of the Queen's (now the King's) peace. Some people think of the criminal law as being a dispute between two people – the 'offender' and the 'victim;' this is not true. That is more akin to a matter in tort for damages, say for assault. The matter is actually between the state and the alleged offender; with the alleged negative actions/omissions towards the 'victim' merely being the conduit by which the state may take action. This is another reason why we don't allow for the victims of crime to choose the punishment of a defendant who is found guilty (a claim I've heard many a populist utter as the ideal method). This is because the 'victim' is actually pretty well removed from the process of an individual defendant against the state's prosecution.

Just a side note – we don't call the person making a criminal complaint a 'victim' at the beginning of a complaint. We call them the 'complainant' (i.e. the person making the criminal complaint). I will discuss this further in the book – but I have extreme scepticism in the way we have (as a society – especially within the media) changed the way in referring to those who make a criminal complaint. The term 'victim' (or 'survivor' – another common term), prior to any finding of guilt, significantly diminishes the ability for a fair trial to be conducted.

More will be spoken on this later.

B *The Burden and Standard of Proof*

The defence in a criminal trial need not (almost always) prove a single thing – they must merely stop the prosecution from showing *every* element of an offence to the required standard of proof.

The prosecution, to gain a conviction, must prove *every* element of an offence 'beyond a reasonable doubt.' This essentially means that if there is a reasonable chance that even one tiny element of an offence (some offences contain many components) is not as the prosecution says – the accused is entitled to acquittal (getting off).

There are a few (very few) exceptions to this.

Sometimes the accused, in the showing of certain defences (for example), will need to prove something to their own standard; note again that this is rather rare. The standard for the defence is (even in the rare exceptions listed above) universally far lower; being the 'balance of probabilities' (50 percent plus one).

An acquittal does not mean an accused person is innocent, it merely means that they are 'not guilty.' Every person in Australia (and every other civilised nation) is deemed innocent until proven guilty. There are very compelling reasons why this is the case, the accused is but one person with very limited resources to mount a defence – this is up against the bottomless pit wielded by the state. The high proof required is partly to balance the score between the two parties. Continuing with this reasoning, as citizens of a western liberal democracy – the value which we (should) hold most dear is individual freedom and liberty; to not be arbitrarily constrained by the government.

Prison and other criminal punishment are forms of violence against you; either you as a person (through imprisonment) or your property (fines as an example). For the state to use violence against you - they better have a bloody good reason to do so, and hence the high standard of proof exists solely on the shoulders of the prosecution. The right to silence is also granted for this reason – namely that the defence need not prove a single thing, and hence, they need not provide any explanation when interrogated. They are innocent at this stage, and thereby it is not for them to show why they aren't guilty.

But for this protection, how many innocents would be punished needlessly?

Also remember that every time an innocent citizen is locked away, the real perpetrator remains walking the streets. That is not to say innocent individuals do not get punished already. During my time working within the criminal field, I worked on a few cases whereby we were attempting to overturn what we (myself and the defence barrister whom I was working for), considered to be wrongful convictions. I remember all these facts clearly, though I am bound by confidentiality so that I may not share them with you here. I will say, however, that I was not only convinced that a decent proportion of the individuals whom we worked for were in the 'not guilty' category – but for some cases I am sure they were innocent. The evidence we looked through, for example, would sometimes almost prove, in my mind at least, the accused *could not* (as opposed to *did not*) have committed the crime. Very confronting to say the least. This is what appeals are for. There are many, many such cases, in which a jury convicts at trial, the first appellate judge upholds the conviction, the court of appeal upholds the conviction again, and then the High Court acquits.

This is what makes our system so resilient – the presumption of innocence *but for* a positive finding of guilt in a court – and that this finding of guilt may then be appealed to another. It is for this reason we trust our court system and believe in its rulings. Any erosion of this trust in justice will *fundamentally* change the way we view our society – just look at the way we view the justice systems under the mid-20th century totalitarian regimes (or North Korea today).
The way to hell is having a low trust society, a society in which its citizens do not trust the governmental structures, nor each other. The way to having a low trust society is having a justice system which nobody trusts or believes in. The way we have that is if innocent people get punished for stuff they didn't do.

On a slight tangent, it is for this reason I am against the death penalty. Even leaving the moral arguments aside - such as that we as a people shouldn't be involved in butchery, or that government fiat doesn't give the right to end life not in self-defence, or that it's always wrong to kill a person with no means to defend themselves. Leaving all this aside, we sometimes get it wrong. Just google, 'wrongful executions,' and be ashamed at how many times an innocent person died, only to be exonerated when it is too late. If this doesn't change your mind on executions; that a system enabling the murder of innocent people is wrong, I don't really know what to say. Imagine how frightened you'd be, or how frightened your kids would be; knowing that this was their last day on earth despite not having committed the crime they were accused of. That to me is unconscionable to the point of repugnancy, that someone could support a system that they know will *inevitably* (even if it's one in a thousand executions) cause someone to be treated as an animal, to slaughter, for a crime they did not do.

I will end with this final statement on costs. If you think executing people is the cheaper alternative to imprisonment; you are dead wrong. The latter is many, many, times cheaper. Effectively, in my mind, you are supporting a more expensive and deeply immoral system if you are for capital punishment.

C Parts of an Offence

There are two components to an offence; the act itself (*actus reus*) and the mental component (*mens rea*). The actus reus is more straight forward. That is, did the accused voluntarily do the thing required for the offence to be committed. Their hands weren't held by another, they aren't involuntarily intoxicated, weren't suffering from certain mental conditions, the action wasn't a reflex (reflexes are interesting as far as the law is concerned), and the accused wasn't under duress - among other factors. I'll give an example here for illustrative purposes. The accused shoots a gun and someone dies. Did they press the trigger themselves willingly? Did someone else press the trigger for them? Did they get startled by a loud noise (and by reflex) pulled the trigger? Were they having a mental breakdown from trauma experiences in war/torture and had no control over their actions? Did someone slip a drug into their drink so that they were so intoxicated they (again) had no control over themselves? Legally speaking, only the first category is certainly a voluntary act. Arguments can also be made over the third depending on surrounding circumstances (as I said, reflexes are legally rather interesting).

The *mens rea*, however, is more complicated, with different offences requiring differing levels of mental involvement with the acts. A basic list is given below with the most fundamental levels of mental awareness and an oversimplified explanation for each category.

(a) Intent: The highest level; actually wanting an event to occur. E.g. Shooting an individual and *wanting* to kill them by doing so.

(b) *Recklessness:* Having a *subjective* foresight of the possibility (foresight of probability in murder) that your actions would complete the offense. E.g. Shooting someone and foreseeing the possibility they would be killed by your actions.

(c) *Negligence:* Did you fall short of the *objective* standard of reasonableness in your behaviour? An example is given in driving an automobile with your eyes closed and injuring someone due to this (despite never actually intending to hurt someone). Because this (clearly) falls short of the objectively reasonable standard for driving behaviour; you are culpable if the legislation/common law states criminal negligence is punishable.

Also note now that the criminal law is reticent to make ordinary negligence criminally punishable. This is because human beings are not perfect. Every single human being on earth has made mistakes from time-to-time. The law is therefore hesitant to make criminal something which we have all done; merely because the consequences of that action have been bad. This is the fundamental difference between utilitarian and deontological ethics. Intent matters within the classically liberal tradition.

I would argue some of the worst changes to the criminal law within recent years has been the creation of new offences, or changing pre-existing offences, to continually erode the requirement of intent to gain criminal convictions.

As hinted above, the criminal legislation or common law precedent will state what level of *mens rea* is required for a particular act to be criminal. Most legislation will expressly state what level of intention is required; likewise the common law precedent will have its own rules on the same subject. Issues arise, however, when legislation is passed which encompasses something that the common law either has not previously considered illegal or is codifying the law and omits to mention the required level of *mens rea* required. As a general rule, the more serious the possible punishment; the higher the standard of intent needed to receive a conviction. The three possible types of offences are:

(a) *Complete Mens Rea:* Those needing a complete examination of *mens rea* by the prosecution at whatever level (be it recklessness, full intent etc.). Note that this is different from the type of *mens rea* required by the offence; merely that an examination of *mens rea* is needed (at all) by the prosecution.

(b) *Strict Liability Offences:* Offences without a *mens rea* component. However, this is blunted by the fact that liability may be removed by the 'honest and reasonable mistake of fact' defence. Basically, the defence is summarised as, if you honestly and reasonably (essentially meaning negligence is excluded) believe that the facts were different to what they actually were, and this leads you to complete an offence; you are acquitted from liability.

(c) *Absolute Liability:* The most harsh form – if you do the act, regardless of whether you intended to do it or not, you are guilty. Even the 'honest and reasonable mistake of fact' defence from above will do nothing to prevent guilt from being established if the *actus reas* is made out.

Now for obvious strategic reasons, when cases revolve around whether the crime contains a *mens rea* component; the defence will argue for a complete *mens rea* assessment and the prosecution will attempt to remove it. The leading case here is '*He Kaw Teh;*' basically some guy claimed he didn't know drugs (a lot of them) were in his bags when going through the airport. Because of the huge quantity of narcotics being trafficked, he was sentenced to life imprisonment at trial. The case revolved (at appeal) around whether the crime was a full *mens rea* or strict liability offence, as the legislation was incredibly vague. The high court struck down the previous judgment and inserted her own. The ruling from the court was that where the legislation is vague on *mens rea*, but the punishments are severe (i.e. imprisonment), the court will assume there was little chance (it is up to the prosecution to prove it) the parliament intended to make the offence strict liability.[48] Hence, full *mens rea* applied, and the gentleman was free to go. The Chief Justice emphasised three points which would aid in the statutory interpretation process:[49]

(a) *Words:* The starting point of any statutory interpretation exercise – should the words expressly state the offence is strict liability against full *mens rea*, the exercise ends.

---

[48] *He Kaw Teh v The Queen* (1985) 157 CLR 523, 529-30.
[49] Ibid.

(b) Purpose: Should the interpretation of a strict liability offence aid in the enforcement of the law – this will tend to showcase the offence limiting a *mens rea* requirement. I will ask a rhetorical question here. How does making an individual who doesn't know drugs are in his bags, liable for drug trafficking, aid in enforcement? Well, clearly, it doesn't.

(c) Seriousness of the Offence: This is basically what is written above; the more serious an offence (and punishment) the higher the likelihood of it being judged as requiring full *mens rea*.

D *Moral Crusades & The Erosion of Innocence*

In recent decades we've had many crusades against those who are alleged to have committed different types of offences – and against defendants generally. From the war against drugs in the latter 20th century, to the war on terror post the 11th of September 2001, to the war against the 'bikies' in my home state of New South Wales in the early 2010's, to the 'one-punch' laws, to the #metoo era of recent years. Each of these eras brought with it challenges to the criminal justice system and a targeted erosion upon the presumption of innocence for certain types of defendant. We've had the bail reforms (of 2013)[50] which attempted to increase the propensity to hold defendants on remand (being incarcerated despite no finding of guilt yet being found – i.e. only being charged, but not yet guilty, of an offense).

We've had changes to the right to silence, arguably the most sacred of the rights of a criminal defendant, allowing the jury to make an 'unfavourable inference' against a defendant if they chose silence during official interrogation (in certain instances).[51]

The most recent crusade in Australia (and in the Western World generally) is that against sexual assault and harassment. While some of the outcomes of this have been favourable – some very 'not nice' (understatement) and high-profile people have been proven (in courts across the Western World) to be guilty of heinous acts. However, other changes to the society and legal system are almost certainly negative.

---

[50] *Bail Act 2013* (NSW).
[51] *Evidence Act 1995* (NSW) s 89A.

Should perpetrators of such offences be punished? Yes.

Do the complainants have the right to redress and voice grievances if they so choose? Also, undoubtably yes.

The issue I find here, however, is twofold.

1 *Innocence*

Simply stating someone did something, to someone else, immediately means roughly half of the listening population believes them - all of this without any shred of proof. I don't want to live in a society mirroring 'Salem' whereby witches are put on trial and burned at the stake for baseless accusations. Allowing any accusation (often from decades past – which also necessarily degrades the veracity of evidence by erosion of memory) to ruin a career or deprive someone of liberty via the criminal sanction does not seem to be the fairest of systems we can create.

We have a better system than Nazi Germany, or the USSR, or North Korea precisely because we do not have that here. We in the Western World have been moving towards a fairer justice system for as long as there was a Western World. Since Rome, we in the West, have held that the burden of proof rests on the person trying to prove a fact – not the person negating it. This is the core of the presumption of innocence. In the original Latin - *Ei incumbit probatio qui dicit, non qui negat.*

The media is by far the worst offender. Every time someone is accused of a heinous crime – you can almost recite the exact stream of events that occur. First the media shows the defendants face and name on TV and in print, then they detail the exact version of events as listed by the complainant (they are often not referred to as the 'complainant' – as a side note), and then some commentators will claim our society is horrid for these things to still occur (implying that the accusations are true). If the defendant is found guilty – no punishment is ever harsh enough (arguably damaging the impartiality of the sentencing process). If they are found not guilty, or a finding of guilt is removed on appeal, then we get some commentators stating that reform of the justice system must occur to ensure an increase in conviction rates. On and on it goes.

From the legal perspective – this is deeply damaging to the presumption of innocence. There are no types or shades or grades of innocence. There is just innocent. The accused is innocent until they are found guilty. They are just as innocent as anyone else in the courtroom. They are just as innocent as the police officer who arrested them - until the very moment they are pronounced guilty. Until that moment, or the moment after they are successful in appeal – they are as innocent (and legally pure) as freshly driven snow.

In the social media age, where we are bombarded by news all the time, I am deeply sceptical of the ability for an accused to receive a fair trial in the face of an unending stream of media, which (at the very least), questions the presumption of innocence.

Not only is this harmful to justice by itself, but it can also undermine the likelihood of a conviction 'sticking' in some circumstances. Trials of this nature can be delayed (and have been delayed) if the media is too intense. It is a ground of appeal. If the media scrutiny (or social commentary generally) of a case is so high and/or so unfavourable to the accused, that a court finds it undermined a fair trial, convictions can be overturned (and have been overturned) on appeal.

Impartial courts, by their nature, are the only place an accused person can receive fair treatment. Courts with their trained lawyers, trained judges, and properly informed juries are the only place that an accused should be put on trial. Everywhere else is (such as in media or in less formal investigative bodies such as those of workplaces and/or places of education) fundamentally unequipped to treat with these matters with the degree of care, fairness, and formality that their seriousness requires. Anything less can be argued to be an afront to justice and the system we have built for thousands of years.

2 *Unfair Systems*

Along with the change in media treatment in these types of cases – there has also been a correspondent change in the legal processes which also have been argued to undermine a fair trial.

There have been proposals (across the 'free' [for now] world) to remove the right of cross examination, alter the types of evidence that may be accepted, give strong warnings to juries about what they may think about certain types of evidence, to remove juries entirely for these types of offences, to change the standard of proof required, and to change the *mens rea* necessary to secure a conviction.

I would argue for *extreme* caution and hesitancy whenever something like this is proposed. Every change which increases the conviction rate, also (by necessity), increases the rates at which innocent individuals are put to the mercy of the criminal sanction – and have their liberty removed.

I'm a libertarian to my bones. I believe in individual freedom. I believe in fair trials. I believe in fair trials for my worst enemies – terrorists, child molesters, murderers, and all those in between. We, as a society, do not know what Pandora's box we are opening if we remove the presumption of innocence, the right to test evidence with *sharp* cross examination, that offences should have full *mens rea* requirements, the right to trial by jury of one's peers, and that guilt needs to be established beyond *all* reasonable doubt for *every* element of the alleged offense.

I argue that we remember who we are in the West and what we value.

We have valued individual liberty above all else. We should continue to value individual liberty above all else.

E *Homicide*

The crime everybody immediately thinks of when criminal law is mentioned. For this reason, we'll start with murder.

The starting point is the legislation;[52] the summarised version being any voluntary act or omission <u>causing</u> death – this is the *actus reus*. The *mens rea* is split into four options:

(a) *Intent*: Having the purpose to kill when committing the act. This is the most straight forward. If I shoot you in the chest and I am trying to kill you by doing so (and you die), I am guilty of murder.

(b) *Intent GBH*: Having the intent to impart 'grievous bodily harm' when committing the act. Slightly more complicated, yet not overly so. Basically if I shoot you, with the intent to seriously hurt you (but not kill you) and you die. I am still guilty of murder. So let's say I shoot you in the leg to seriously hurt you, and you bleed out as a result – I am guilty of murder. GBH has a more fleshed out legal definition; this will be dealt with more thoroughly in the assault section of the book.

(c) *Reckless Indifference*: Having the subjective foresight that death was 'probable' as a result of your actions. This is probably (pun intended) the most complicated subheading for *mens rea*. This is basically recklessness, but with the addition of foresight of 'probability' as opposed to 'possibility.' Whether the accused foresaw this (or any *mens rea* requirement) is a matter for the trier of fact to determine (i.e. the jury if one is employed). The leading case of *Crabbe*[53] had this being answered in the affirmative when the offender drove a big truck through a building (and killed people in the process). In *Royall*[54] the court added a New South Wales specification; the foresight must only be to death and not grievous bodily harm – so in certain other states should you have a foresight of GBH (but not death) you are still guilty of murder. In New South Wales however, the foresight must be to death being probable. The same case also makes the method of death becoming nigh irrelevant. Here the offender made threats (i.e. assaulted) to the victim. The unique facts here are that the threats never

---

[52] *Crimes Act 1900* (NSW) s 18.
[53] *R v Crabbe* (1985) 156 CLR 464.
[54] *Royall v The Queen* (1991) 172 CLR 378.

materialised as the victim jumped out of a window and died. The issue was whether the offender (who foresaw the chance of death as a result of his threats) was equally liable for the victim's death being the result of falling from a height. The court answered in the affirmative, once you foresee the probability of death, as long as the *actus reus* remains intact (the chain of causation) – you are liable. Because of this, the case is also used as a paradigm in the law of causation as well.

(d) Constructive Murder: Just note if you see the term 'felony murder' in older judgments, they are talking about this. If you are committing a crime that has a maximum penalty of 25 (or more) years – and someone dies (due to a voluntary action or omission) either during the commission of the crime, or immediately after, you are guilty of the crime (murder) without any discussion of *mens rea*. Here, liability (for murder) is absolute, meaning once the *actus reus* is established, you are guilty. Of course, the *mens rea* for the initial crime (say an armed robbery) need be made out. Because of the absolute liability, defences here invariably revolve around the *actus reus* of a crime – it is here that the law of 'reflexes' becomes interesting (as previously noted). The most well-known case of constructive murder is *Ryan*,[55] here an armed robbery was taking place and the offender shot the gun on reflex from being startled. The issue was whether this was a voluntary act or not, being paramount to the existence (or not) of the required *actus reus*. The court interpreted the act as being distinct from the physical pulling of the trigger. The voluntary act needed for murder was changed from firing the gun to something akin to presenting a loaded firearm in a manner that it could have been fired. Because this was certainly voluntary, the offender was convicted for murder.

The *actus reus* for murder is a little less segmented; that being an act or omission causing death.[56]

(a) An Act: Any voluntary act – hence the *Ryan*[57] issue above is also relevant. This is the most simplistic issue to be discussed here.

---

[55] *Ryan v The Queen* (1967) 121 CLR 205.
[56] *Crimes Act 1900* (NSW) s 18.
[57] *Ryan v The Queen* (1967) 121 CLR 205.

(b) *An Omission:* An omission, something that was not done (yet ought to have been done). Because imposing a legal obligation of care onto another is so onerous a burden on individual liberty (you are generally not obliged to save a stranger from drowning for example – even a child); the law only imposes such a 'duty of care' in certain instances. The leading case of *Taktak*[58] within Australia outlines four possibilities in which this may be shown:

   (i) *Statutory Duty:* Where legislation makes it clear you have a duty of care – a duty of care exists. An example is 'section 44 of the *I just made this up Act.*' Section 44 of this fictional legislation states that all police officers shall have responsibility for all children playing on swings. Any police officer who then sees a child in distress on a swing and does nothing (and the child dies somehow) is guilty (should all other factors of the crime be met). Any nurse, fireman, police officer, doctor, teacher, and other like professions are (or should be) well aware of their statutory duties.

   (ii) *Contractual Duty:* Pretty obvious – you sign (or otherwise make) a contact saying you have a duty of care to another person.

   (iii) *Relationship Based Duty:* The kid drowning is my child, or my ward, or my friend's kid and we decided I'd take care of him/her for the day etc. Any relationship in which you have (by nature of the relationship) a duty to care for another.

   (iv) *Voluntary Assumption of care PLUS seclusion:* You find someone who is having a seizure on the floor and you then take them to your house to care for them. You do a bad job at caring for them and they die. Because you voluntarily chose to care for that person, and moved them into a position in which someone else could not care for them (by taking them into your private house) – you are deemed responsible for them.

---

[58] *R v Taktak* (1988) 14 NSWLR 226.

(c) Causation: Your act or omission must actually cause the death. Let me give you an example; you shoot someone and leave them to die. Instead of the bullet killing them, they stumble off a balcony (using similar facts as *Royall*) and the fall kills them, did you cause it? Clearly we can have different formulae for this determination:

(i) *Direct Causation Necessity:* Should we make the test of causation too narrow and state that the direct action of yours must cause the death – then guilt would be evaded in the above example. This is because even in the scenario where their stumbling (from being shot) causes them to fall off the edge, it remains the height (and the force of gravity) that did the killing instead of you.

(ii) *Overly Broad:* Let's now suppose your bullet did nothing to them, it skimmed off their shin and the person was fine. They then went camping a few days later, got drunk, and fell off a cliff while intoxicated – all whilst trying to look at the scab you have caused. Should we make the test of causation so broad as to include something akin to 'any action of our own that may have aided in death' then you would be guilty of murder.

Even in this admittedly silly example, it is easy to observe that a balance need be struck between an overly narrow and artificially broad definition. The courts have struggled with this for decades in formulating the ideal method of determination. The most widely accepted formula (in NSW at least) seems to be from *Royall*[59] (the window case from above). The case effectively holds that so long as the accused's actions were an 'operating and substantial' cause of the death – they are liable (with the other murder requirements being met). In *Royall*[60] therefore, the deceased's actions in jumping from the window were caused (substantially) by the assault. This (whether you substantially caused the death or not) is for the trier of fact to determine – the jury; should one exist. The issue may then arise in special cases where some 'special vulnerability' affecting the deceased (and not the general public) may be blamed for the death – what then? An illustration of this can be given (in an example) in which you stab someone; and the stab is merely on their leg. A normal person would most likely survive, but because the victim suffers from some inherited disorder making them more vulnerable – they die.

---

[59] *Royall v The Queen* (1991) 172 CLR 378.
[60] Ibid.

The short answer to this issue of causation is known as the 'egg shell skull rule.' Effectively the principle states that anyone using violence on another can't rely on any weakness of the victim to escape full liability. If someone has a special condition and they happen to die by your actions because of it; you're guilty. The English case of *Blaue*[61] is the paradigm example of this principle. Here the victim's religion stopped them from receiving the blood transfusion which would have saved their life (post a violent crime). Despite the victim's own choice (in refusing the blood) leading to their demise – the offender was still held responsible for the death.

The issue of medical treatment may then arise – namely can medical treatment be so bad that the chain of causation is broken? In short; medical treatment must be reckless (not negligent) to break the causal chain. So let's return to the stabbing analogy (you stab someone). In the course of their medical treatment for the stab wound, the medical staff ought to have noticed the wound becoming infected (but they didn't notice) and hence the victim soon dies of sepsis. You would still remain liable for the death as the actions of the medical staff were merely negligent – i.e. they did not meet the objective standard of reasonableness they should have. This is contrasted to a situation whereby all medical staff foresee a possibility the wound becoming infected and then continue doing nothing. Here the recklessness of the medical staff is enough to break the causal chain and for you to 'get off.' Naturally, you'd still be liable for assault (probably assault causing GBH – we'll speak about what this is in the section below).

Manslaughter is slightly different; with two sub-categories. Involuntary manslaughter involves a homicide without the requisite intention for a murder. Voluntary manslaughter refers to cases in which the requisite intent is founded, yet the offence is downgraded to manslaughter due to other factors (such as the existence of certain partial defences). The following section will detail *highly* summarised versions of the two types of involuntary manslaughter. Also note that the causation rules (as above) continue to apply.

(a) *Dangerous & Unlawful Act:* A voluntary and *unlawful* (another crime of some species, generally an assault) act of the accused being intentionally performed. This act also needs to be so dangerous that the reasonable person (in the accused's position) would

---

[61] *R v Blaue* (1975) 61 Cr App R 271.

be aware they were revealing the victim to harm.[62] The crux of this issue generally revolves around what the reasonable person would have been aware of. For the purposes of this analysis, the reasonable person is judged to be of the same age,[63] yet with other characteristics such as intoxication not included. Disability (if relevant) can be included.

(b) *Criminal Negligence:* Where the accused's actions fell so far from the standard, of a reasonable person, where the risk of death/GBH is so high; that these actions deserve the criminal sanction.[64] Note now that the degree of negligence must be very, very high, to warrant criminal punishment for manslaughter.

F *Assault*

Again, the starting point of our analysis, is the legislation. Here the most basic form of assault (common assault) is defined by the statute,[65] as being merely the act itself - an assault. This is without the extra circumstances of the further assault offences; namely the weapons used or the degree of damage to the victim which are to be explained below. The number one rule of definitions is to not use the very word you are defining in your explanation – yet the legislation does this without remorse. The common law is therefore left to discern what an assault is. This isn't really a problem however, considering the judge made definition existed well before the legislation (or even the nation of Australia) entered existence.

1 *Actus Reus*

The acts required for an assault can be split in twain (either of the following can constitute the necessary *actus reus*):

---

[62] *Wilson v The Queen* (1992) 174 CLR 313, 333.
[63] *DPP v TY* (2006) 167 A Crim R 596.
[64] *Nydam v The Queen* [1977] VR 430, 445.
[65] *Crimes Act 1900* (NSW) s 61.

(a) *Non-Physical:* The offender creates, in the mind of the victim, an apprehension of immediate and unlawful contact.[66] So you stand over someone and make a threat that you are going to punch them in the face (without actually doing so). This is an assault.

(b) *Physical (battery):* The offender actually applying such unlawful contact to the victim – such as punching them in the face.[67]

Just note that unlawful, in this context, usually means any contact without consent. Consent negates the assault from existing (hence why boxing with a referee, as an example, is not illegal).

In the English jurisdiction (Australia follows this) there is a threshold of harm above which you cannot consent. The leading case here, that every law student is well aware of, is *Brown*.[68] The matter surrounded a group of men who consented to, and performed on each other, a whole bunch of sadomasochistic acts in which bodily harm was inflicted. The court concluded that the high degree of harm inflicted negated the consent.[69] This is contrasted to something like rough 'horseplay' by male friends – which you can legally consent to.[70]

2 *Mens rea*

(a) *Intent:* The offender intends to apply that unlawful force, or intends to raise the immediate fear of unlawful contact.[71]

(b) *Recklessness:* The offender foresees the possibility their actions would raise the fear of unlawful contact but continues to do so.[72] The same is true for actually imparting the unlawful force.

---

[66] *R v Burstow; R v Ireland* [1998] 1 AC 147.
[67] *Darby v DPP* (NSW) (2004) 150 A Crim R 314, 328.
[68] *R v Brown* [1994] 1 AC 212.
[69] Ibid (Lord Templeman).
[70] *R v Jones* [1987] Crim LR 123.
[71] *R v Savage; DPP v Parmenter* [1992] 1 AC 699.
[72] Ibid.

3 Special Types of Assault

We've dealt with the paradigm case – now we deal with the additions to the basic crime. Please note that these typically the relevant penalties to be found.

> *(a) Actual Bodily Harm:* An assault which causes 'actual bodily harm.'[73] Again we find the problem of using the defined word within the explanation. The common law has its own definition – some harm inflicted on the body which impacts health, the type of treatment received, and whether functions of the body were affected in some way.[74] The penalties are further increased if you commit this crime in the presence of others.[75] This is a common thread in assault law; generally there will be a duplicate offense with greater sanction should the offence occur in the company of others. The reasoning here is rather clear, we as a society view gang related violence as particularly reprehensible (as the victim has a lesser chance of self-defence, as coupled with the generally higher propensity for harm).
>
> *(b) Wounding:* Defined by the common law (again the legislation makes no attempt to do so) as an assault breaking the skin.[76] Now there are a whole bunch of crimes listed for wounding – caused recklessly,[77] the same in company,[78] with intent to cause GBH/resist arrest[79] etc. There are simply too many to go through each in more detail than simply the list above; just note there is a bunch of them.
>
> *(c) Grievous Bodily Harm:* The legislation defines GBH as permanent/serious disfiguring, killing a foetus, and any grievous bodily disease.[80] The common law defines it (the word grievous) as very serious harm.[81] Again we have a whole bunch of offences which have the infliction of GBH as their central theme. Recklessly causing it,[82] the same in company,[83] inflicting it with intent to cause GBH or resist arrest.[84]

---

[73] *Crimes Act 1900* (NSW) s 59.
[74] *Wayne v Boldiston* (1992) 62 A Crim R 1, 7-8.
[75] *Crimes Act 1900* (NSW) s 59(2).
[76] *Vallance v The Queen* (1961) 108 CLR 56.
[77] *Crimes Act 1900* (NSW) s 35(4).
[78] Ibid (3)
[79] Ibid s 33(1)-(2).
[80] Ibid s 4(1).
[81] *Haoui v R* (2008) 188 A Crim R 331 [137].
[82] *Crimes Act 1900* (NSW) s 35(2).
[83] Ibid (1).
[84] Ibid s 33(1)-(2).

(d) *Weapons:* If you use a firearm or any other loaded 'at range' type weapon with the intent to cause GBH[85] or to resist arrest[86] – there are extra penalties here. There are other offences for merely possessing certain types of weapons.

(e) *One-Punch Legislation:* There is now a stand-alone offense for assaults causing death whereby an assault is committed with any part of the body or any instrument held by the offender and this causes death.[87] Do this crime while intoxicated (and over 18 years of age) and you will find a greater maximum penalty (25 years instead of 20)[88] and with a mandatory minimum sentence of eight years.[89] There has been heavy criticism of the mandatory minimum here by more libertarian leaning individuals. The role of the sentencing judge has been argued as being artificially constrained by the legislation – becoming more akin to a clerk applying the relevant spreadsheet as opposed to the formulation of an applicable sentence using all relevant factors of the case. Proponents will claim this provides an extra disincentive to engage in alcohol fuelled violence.

G Sexual Assault

1 Actus Reus

As a preliminary point – the term 'sexual assault' is the phrase within criminal law used when referring to rape. I only note this because it can easily be confused with something akin to 'unwanted groping' which is (or was – explained below) an indecent assault.[90] Since writing this book – indecent assault has now turned to 'sexual touching.'

The legislation is rather concise here – any non-consented to sexual intercourse.[91] The statue then defines the meaning of sexual intercourse to effectively include any penetration by anything of the mouth, genitals, and anus.[92] Consent is defined as a 'free and voluntary'

---

[85] Ibid s33A(1).
[86] Ibid (2).
[87] Ibid s25A(1).
[88] Ibid (2).
[89] Ibid s 25B(1).
[90] Ibid s 61L.
[91] Ibid s 61I.
[92] Ibid s 61H.

agreement.[93] Just note there are aggravated forms of this basic offense (with higher penalties) including inflicting actual bodily harm, threatening behaviour, the offense occurring in company, the victim being under 16 years of age (or having a serious disability), depriving the victim of liberty, and also breaking and entering before the incident (with intent to commit a serious indictable offence).[94] There is another, even higher form of this offence whereby the aggravated form is performed (ABH, threatening behaviour, and depriving liberty) in company.[95]

Regarding consent, there are a few important factors which may negate this 'free and voluntary agreement,' including but not limited to (the full list will be in the reference) consent given under threat, detainment, mistaken identity (must be the exact identity and not characteristics of the person i.e. the fact that the complainant was under a mistaken belief as to the accused's wealth, status, occupation, and other factors are irrelevant),[96] and other[97] factors.

What is very interesting to note, is that the 'intoxication' negation of consent may lead to some unwanted impositions of liability in certain instances. It is clear that should one sober, or more sober individual, 'take advantage' of another intoxicated individual - this is a very deserving place for liability. However, the law does not currently place exception for the circumstance in which BOTH parties were equally and heavily intoxicated. Because the law makes no allowance for self-induced intoxication (discussed later in the book), sexual intercourse between two very intoxicated individuals creates a situation in which they have legally sexually assaulted each other. That is, they may both may be liable (guilty) in this circumstance.

2 Mens rea

The legislation also makes clear the intent required for liability to be imparted under this section. The initial wording suggests only knowledge will be sufficient for guilt – however 'knowledge' is later expanded to include recklessness regarding consent[98] (including inadvertent recklessness – meaning the offender not turning their mind to the issue of consent

---

[93] Ibid s 61HA(2).
[94] Ibid s 61J.
[95] Ibid s 61JA.
[96] *Papadimitropoulos v The Queen* (1957) 98 CLR 249, 254.
[97] *Crimes Act 1900* (NSW) s 61HA(4)-(8).
[98] Ibid (3).

at all).[99] Recent legislative change has also moved liability outside a purely subjective inquiry to include whether or not there were any reasonable grounds to believe consent had been given.[100] Just note the 'reasonableness' inquiry is not that of the 'reasonable person' but instead an inquiry into the accused's state of mind (i.e. were there any reasonable grounds from the position of the accused).[101]

There have been even more recent changes occurring in the last few years. The state of New South Wales has now moved to an 'affirmative' consent requirement for all sexual offences. They have also changed the names of various offences – e.g. sexual touching (instead of indecent assault). Other states have also followed (and yet more are still in the process of following).

The main change is to *mens rea,* meaning that there will not be reasonable grounds to believe consent was present if the accused did not, within a reasonable timeframe, ensure consent was present. This change was conducted for numerous reasons – one of which was a response to low conviction rates for these types of offences.

These changes were met with extreme controversy from the legal fraternity – with many high-profile lawyers speaking against such changes. I don't think I can do better than an assessment from the NSW Bar Association, so I've included the article *'Consent Proposals Could Result in Significant Injustice,'* alongside my analysis of this change in the law. The full version of the article is in this footnote.[102] Just note the hyperlink I've put in works as of the 25th of December 2022 (yes, it is Christmas Day when writing this – Merry Christmas). If it doesn't work when you try to find the article, I'm sure google will assist you just by including the name of the article (and having 'NSW Bar Association') in your search.

There are many issues to speak about regarding these changes.

As a side note – I will be giving reasonably graphic descriptions of scenarios in the following section. I only do this because there's no other way to communicate precisely what these changes may mean without giving examples.

---

[99] *Gillard v The Queen* (2014) 88 ALJR 606 [26]; *R v Kitchener* (1993) 29 NSWLR 696.
[100] *Crimes Act 1900* (NSW) s 61HA(3)(c).
[101] *O'Sullivan v R; Flanders v R; Tohu v R & NRH v R* [2012] NSWCCA 45 [124].
[102] New South Wales Bar Association, *'Media Release: Consent Proposals Could Result in Significant Injustice,'* (Web Page, 26 May 2021) <https://nswbar.asn.au/the-bar-association/publications/inbrief/view/08b347d11316f1372f3414b4c466afe4>.

1 *First Moves*

These changes don't merely apply to sexual assault (rape). They also apply to most other activities within the full spectrum of intimate physical relations. That first innocent 'touch on the lap and stroke of the leg' to let the other person know you are interested (on a first/second date for example) – is now possibly illegal. The act of slowly sliding one's hand down your partner's back, whilst kissing, and then squeezing their bottom (which is present in every single Hollywood romcom) is now almost certainly illegal in New South Wales. The moving of a hand underneath the covers, in bed, to arouse your longstanding partner (even if married) whilst watching a movie and without saying a word – is now definitely illegal. Even if one is in a committed relationship with another – if consent is not asked prior to physical activity being conducted – it is illegal.

If you want to make people, particularly young people (and especially men/boys), *terrified* of starting sexual encounters – this is how you do it.

Love is hard at any age. It is especially hard when you are young.

2 *Every Activity Needs Consent*

One of the biggest changes to the law is that *every single specific act* needs to have consent. Let's say one person is kissing another, they then move their hands down to the buttocks and squeeze – if consent on the squeeze is not given beforehand – it is illegal. Even if this exact activity has been done thousands of times before in the context of a longstanding relationship, every single time it is done, it requires fresh consent otherwise an assault will most likely have (legally) been committed. Touching the breasts, genitals, and so forth, is the same – each requiring fresh consent. Every. Single. time.

If sexual intercourse is being had, and one person touches another part of the other (e.g. scrotum, breasts, etc) – this also requires consent prior to it being performed. Otherwise an assault may possibly (legally) have been committed. The act of sex (to be legal) becomes a series of questions from both parties – losing all humanity and becoming about as dreary as a contract to buy a property.

3 *I thought we needed mens rea?*

For a murder to be a murder, you need intention. For stealing to be stealing – you need intention. For essentially every single serious offense – intention is required before criminal liability may be established. The recent changes, to sexual offences, makes these types of offence unique within the canon of criminal law within a liberal democracy. What happened to the sacred rule that we (as freedom loving citizens of a free country) only punish bad actions *when combined* with bad intentions?

4 *An Incentive for Lying*

There is no way any defendant, when accused of any of these offences, will state that the complainant didn't actively communicate consent. It simply would not be in their interest to do so. The following two defences will likely be the overwhelming majority (even more so than they are currently) going forward:

(a) *No Sexual Activity:* The defendant may claim that there was no sexual activity at all between themselves and the defendant.
(b) *Enthusiastic Consent:* The defendant may claim that they had asked prior to every step of the sexual congress and that enthusiastic consent was given each time.

Where in previous cases the jury would be asked to conduct an inquiry into the state of mind of the accused as to the sexual activity occurred – now it will be even more of a 'he said she said' type scenario (where each party is giving wildly differing versions of events). This may actually make convictions less easy to secure, flimsier on appeal, and generally make it more difficult for juries to wade through the claims being made by each party. There's also the nullification issue to consider – but that's a story for another day.

H *Larceny*

The statute provides little guidance as to the elements of the offence and hence the common law provides her own definition.[103]

1 *Actus Reus*

(a) Tangible Thing: For larceny to exist, you must steal something that can actually be stolen - i.e. tangible chattels. These must also have the ability for some level of ownership, even mere possessory title (and not necessarily complete ownership), to transfer with possession. If it is not a tangible thing – this is where fraud probably comes in (as discussed below).

(b) Property Belongs to Another with Better Title: The property you steal must be sourced from another with better title than your own – i.e. you cannot steal from someone with whom the property in question is more yours than theirs.

(c) Asportation: Any act which actively 'moves' the goods with intent to steal them. Even acts of deception may be enough in certain cases. I know it's slightly uncouth of me, as an Australian lawyer (something I would have gotten into a lot of trouble for in law school), to use an American precedent to prove my point, but the law is pretty much the same here between the two jurisdictions (plus I love old cases). In *Commonwealth v Barry*[104] the accused had switched the labels on a baggage trunk (hence meaning it would be transported to a different place). This was enough to make out the necessary asportation needed for conviction, despite the lacking of a physical 'carrying' act by the offender.

(d) No Consent: This almost need not be in the book – stealing something with consent (from the person owns that thing) is not stealing.

---

[103] *Crimes Act 1900* (NSW) s 117.
[104] 125 Mass. 390 (1878).

2 Mens Rea

(a) *Intention of Permanently Depriving the Owner:* Traditionally, to be guilty of larceny, you must steal (with intention to keep) the thing you are charged of stealing. An example of this can be found in a case we covered extensively in law school (and a serious debate was had in class on whether it was correctly decided) – the case of *Velumyl*.[105] Essentially, the offender took money from the company for which he worked. He then claimed he wanted to repay the same amount of money – and thereby should not be guilty (as he claimed he did not have the requisite intention to permanently deprive the owner). Despite his claim he intended to repay the money, he was found liable.

The reasoning here was that unless he intended to repay the actual/physical notes stolen, this wouldn't properly replace the property – it would instead be merely replacing the notes with something of equivalent value.

To take property with the intention of 'borrowing it' would traditionally be on shaky ground regarding the ability for the prosecution to gain a conviction. Statute has attempted to limit this difficulty, with the legislation expanding this 'permanent depravation' intent, to include a 'borrowing' type act, so long as the accused used the property for their own or another's benefit.[106]

(b) *Dishonesty:* A portion of the offence also requires the stealing to be 'dishonest.' This is placed in there so that neighbours who have known each other for years don't get arrested when one goes to the others house, takes some eggs from the fridge and places a note saying, "I used your eggs, come over for cake later – Sally." There was a whole bunch of precedent with different definitions for dishonesty; this has been cleared through statute. A finding of dishonesty is a matter for the trier of fact, (i.e. jury should there be one) by the standards of ordinary people.[107]

(c) *Claim of Right:* There is a unique defence for larceny. Should the accused have an honest belief, in their legal right to the goods that were taken, they may well be found not guilty.[108] The belief need not be reasonable, merely a subjective test (as a matter for

---

[105] *R v Velumyl* [1989] Crim LR 299.
[106] *Crimes Act 1900* (NSW) s 118.
[107] Ibid s 4B.
[108] *R v Fuge* (2001) 123 A Crim R 310 (Woods CJ).

the trier of fact) that the prosecution has not proved beyond a reasonable doubt, that the accused did not hold such a belief.

3 Additions to the Basic Crime – Robberies and Stealing from the Person

Larceny is the base crime – stealing some tangible good which does not belong to you. The criminal law adds to this foundation with two additional (and more serious) crimes.

- (a) *Robbery:* A robbery[109] contains all the elements of larceny, but with the added elements that the taking of the goods be with violence/assault inflicted to the victim (above what is needed to take the good) and be in their presence.

- (b) *Stealing from the Person:* 'Stealing from the person' is an offence of the same quality, but without the violence – i.e. a non-violent larceny conducted in the presence of the victim.[110]

I *Fraud*

Fraud is rather well articulated by the statute, and while common law principles exist which aid in refining the legislation – the great majority of the offence is easily referenced back to parliament.

1 *Actus Reus*

- (a) *Property and Benefit*: Should someone obtain property belonging to another, cause financial benefit to themselves/another, or cause financial disadvantage to others.[111]

---

[109] *Crimes Act 1900* (NSW) s 94
[110] *R v Delk* (1999) 46 NSWLR 340 [30].
[111] *Crimes Act 1900* (NSW) 192E(1).

(b) *Deception:* The above is done through an act of deception[112] – defined as any deception (any lie or other form of trickery) through words or conduct.[113]

In a world where most forms of property are no longer tangible – fraud is becoming a relatively (when compared to larceny – the stealing of physical goods) more common form of crime.

2 Mens Rea

(a) *Deception:* The deception must be either reckless (foresight of possibility) or intentional.[114]

(b) *Dishonest:* The deception must also be dishonest according to the same standard as larceny.[115]

J Drug Law

This will be an extremely summarised version of a complicated bunch of doctrines. As a starting point we look to the law of possession, the basic offence.

1 Possession

Possession of an illicit substance is the circumstance in which the accused had in their 'physical control' the drug in question. One case we covered extensively in class (and one which often comes up in law school exams) is the leading case of *Filipetti*.[116] In this case the drugs were found in a room (from memory it was a share-house) in which multiple parties had access to. The prosecution found it impossible to disprove the notion the drugs belonged to other members of the house and thereby the accused was found not guilty. This is an example of an

---

[112] Ibid.
[113] Ibid s192B.
[114] Ibid (2).
[115] Ibid s 4B.
[116] *R v Filipetti* (1984) 13 A Crim R 335.

area in which the high standard of proof necessary for the functioning of a free society also increases the propensity for a crime to be committed. The case has been criticised often on the basis that it makes the successful conviction of an individual charged with drug possession nigh impossible should they be stored in plain sight (or at least in a place not within the exclusive control of the accused). The counter here to this criticism is that any other standard of proof would also increase the probability, as a rule of mathematical certainty, that innocent parties within shared living arrangements would be convicted of crimes they simply didn't commit. Just note the *He Kaw Teh*[117] rules from earlier apply, meaning the accused cannot be found guilty of possession had they not known/intended to be in possession of the narcotic. As mentioned already mentioned, this removes the ability for individuals who have drugs placed inside travel bags by others to be found guilty – clearly a benefit to society. The strangest case I've ever seen in court (not a client of the barrister I assisted – this event was seen during public observation of the court for a university assignment) was where the accused had lost their wallet at a music festival. The wallet was subsequently found by police, they searched it, and found within it a single dose of some narcotic. What was interesting about this case is that the accused admitted wrongdoing (i.e. a confession was made regarding ownership of the substance). Had the accused simply said, 'yes this is my wallet, but I have no idea how that got in there,' it is nearly impossible they would have been convicted. This is because the prosecution, in accordance with *Filipetti,* would have no means of proving (to the beyond all reasonable doubt standard) that the narcotics were placed into the accused's wallet by their own hand. This was obviously a very honest person.

Building on the basic crime of possession; should you make, sell, grow, or do anything to aid in the process of the listed categories, the punishments are increased from the initial possession charge. Just note there also exists in the legislation a classification of 'deemed supply,' whereby should the accused be found with over a certain amount of each type of drug, they will be charged for supply of it (as the law deems it unlikely such a quantity was merely for personal use).

---

[117] (1985) 157 CLR 523.

K *Defences - General*

We've now been through the criminal offences which are perhaps most captivating. Due to the short nature of this book, we'll move on now to some of the most important defences. As a preliminary point, note that certain defences are complete – in the sense that they strip liability in its totality. In the alternative, other defences (known as partial defences) strip certain types of liability or downgrade offences to a less severe form.

L *Defence of Intoxication*

The defence is split between self-induced, and non-self-induced intoxication.

(a) Self Induced Intoxication: Self-Induced intoxication is any intoxication not induced by fraud, emergency, accident, reasonable mistake, duress, force, involuntariness, administration by a medical practitioner, and in accordance with your prescription.[118] In summary, self-induced intoxication may negate the *mens rea* for specific intent offences, meaning a self-induced offender escapes liability for their commission.[119]

A specific intent offence is effectively a crime, with which the *mens rea* has (as a necessary component), the intention to cause some particular circumstance. So, an assault is the general offence, an assault with intent to inflict GBH is the specific intent permutation. Self-induced intoxication, as a defence, may remove the ability for the prosecution to gain a conviction for the latter but not the former. As such, the prosecution will be able to convict the accused on the general offence. Murder is another example here, being reduced to manslaughter.[120] A list of these offences (non-exclusive) is provided in the legislation.[121] Also, important to note, is that the defence does not apply should the accused have resolved to commit the crime before intoxication or used intoxication to provide 'Dutch Courage.'[122] Self-induced intoxication is not relevant for the *actus reus* of any offence.[123]

---

[118] *Crimes Act 1900* (NSW) s 428A.
[119] Ibid s 428C.
[120] Ibid s 428E.
[121] Ibid s 428B.
[122] Ibid s 428C(2).
[123] Ibid s 428G(1).

(b) Non-Self Induced: For all other offences (be they specific intent or not), non-self-induced intoxication may be taken into account into the *mens rea* of such offences.[124]

Regarding the *actus reus* of offences, this defence may also be taken into account to negate the voluntariness of such crimes – i.e. you were so drunk or high (being intoxicated not by your own hand) that you had no control over your own actions to the extent that they were not voluntary.[125] Obviously, non-self-induced intoxication mostly refers to spiking incidents.

M *Self Defence*

The legislation identifies in what circumstances an individual may have liability expunged due to self-defence. These categories include the defending of themselves or another, to protect against trespass, and in defending against property interference (I say interference because this is the lowest threshold instance i.e. the other listed categories, in the statute, would also be included as interference).[126] Note the individual must believe the conduct necessary for one or more of the listed reasons.[127] The burden of proof lies on the prosecution to disprove the defence at the beyond a reasonable doubt standard (once raised by the defence at the evidentiary standard).[128] To raise self-defence, the defence must satisfy that there is a relevant nexus between the offence (to be expunged of liability) and the perceived threat.

The other common law refinements on the defence are that:

(a) Subjectively Necessity: A subjective inquiry is used as to whether the accused subjectively believed self-defence was necessary.[129] Most subjective idiosyncrasies of the accused may be taken into account here.

(b) Reasonableness: Just when you thought we escaped an objective test, here we are. The accused must also show that their actions were within the realm of reasonableness from

---

[124] Ibid s 428D.
[125] Ibid s 428G.
[126] Ibid s 418.
[127] Ibid.
[128] Ibid s 419.
[129] *R v Katarzynski* [2002] NSWSC 613 [22]-[23].

the perspective of a reasonable person.[130] Only certain factors of the accused may be analysed here.

The defence also does not apply should the offender recklessly (or intentionally) cause death to protect property or against trespass.[131]

There was once a common law ping-pong game played, regarding liability, in cases of excessive force used in self-defence (leading to death). Some cases had said this was murder, others a form of voluntary manslaughter. This is all meaningless today, as statute has cleared the way, and made clear the voluntary manslaughter (downgrade from murder) alternative is to be preferred. Just note, the conduct must be to protect against bodily integrity – i.e. physical self-defence and not against property (be they chattels or land).[132]

N *Insanity Defence*

Contrary to popular belief, the insanity defence is not a golden ticket. Should you be found insane, you will likely be locked up in a mental health institution for a very long time – often longer than the jail sentence you 'escaped' from. From a practical perspective, it's only worth claiming mental illness, in most cases, should you be charged with murder.

I think we can knock this defence over pretty quickly by reference to the leading and perhaps oldest case. In *M'Naghten*,[133] the judgment can be summarised that every man is deemed sane at first instance and that this presumption may be rebutted as a matter for the trier of fact to determine. The jury must be satisfied (at the lower standard of the 'balance of probabilities') that:

(a) *Disease:* The accused must have been suffering from a 'disease of the mind,' AND

(b) *Nature of Act:* The accused did not know the nature of their act, OR

(c) *Morality:* The accused did not realise their actions were wrong at the time.

---

[130] *Abdallah v R* [2016] NSWCCA 34.
[131] *Crimes Act 1900* (NSW) s 420.
[132] Ibid s 421.
[133] *R v M'Naghten* (1843) 8 ER 718, 722.

Since first writing this book, apparently this common law test has been legislated and is now found in a new statute passed in 2020.[134] The finding/verdict has also been changed from 'not guilty' to 'act proven but not criminally responsible.'[135]

There is another (similar) *partial* defence named 'substantial impairment' whereby the accused (if successful) is suffering from an 'abnormality of the mind,' so substantial, that it warrants a downgrade from murder to voluntary manslaughter.[136] The elements, of such an abnormality of mind, need to impact the following areas within the accused:

(a) *Capacity:* Their ability to understand events, OR

(b) *Control*: Control themselves, OR

(c) *Morality*: Judge right from wrong, AND

(d) The impairment is so substantial that it warrants a downgrade from murder to manslaughter.

Just note it is for the jury to determine whether this is the case. I will also reiterate that the mental defect need be less severe than a 'disease of the mind' (of the insanity defence).

Ironically, sometimes the prosecution will be the party attempting to prove insanity to secure a longer custodial sentence, of one kind or another, and the defence will be attempting to showcase substantial impairment. Again, this is due to a jail sentence for manslaughter maybe being lesser (in time) when compared to an indefinite stint in a mental health hospital.

O *Automatism*

This is arguably the golden ticket that popular culture may assume insanity to be. If the defence proves automatism – i.e. a lack of voluntariness of the actions of the accused, then there will be no scope for incarceration of any type (getting off 'scot free').[137] The defence is somewhat

---

[134] *Mental Health and Cognitive Impairment Forensic Provisions Act 2020* (NSW) s 28.
[135] Ibid s 30.
[136] *Crimes Act 1900* (NSW) s 23A.
[137] *Ryan v The Queen* (1967) 121 CLR 205 [20]-[26]; *Bratty v A-G for Northern Ireland* (1963) AC 386, 409, cited in *Ryan v The Queen* (1967) 121 CLR 205 [20]-[23].

of a double edged sword however, in that the prosecution will almost invariably attempt to portray the actions of the accused as being the result of a 'diseased mind.' Therefore, the same evidence 'of a lack of control' may also aid the prosecution in proving insanity.

As a general rule, conditions likely to recur, and also anything showcasing '*M'Naghten*' type symptoms such as the inability to distinguish right from wrong, will be evidence of insanity. This is contrasted with the conditions of which a reasonable mind would not be able to 'withstand,' not being likely to recur, and also producing the necessary loss of voluntariness - showing evidence of automatism.[138] Sleepwalking is perhaps the paradigm example here.[139]

P *Extreme Provocation*

This was previously a common law partial defence (which did not require the conduct to be an offense) which has now been usurped by statute.

Murder may be downgraded to manslaughter if the jury is satisfied that:[140]

(a) The homicide was in response to the deceased's conduct towards or affecting the accused, AND,

(b) The conduct of the deceased was a serious indictable offence, and

(c) The conduct of the deceased caused the accused to lose self-control, and

(d) The conduct of the deceased could have caused an ordinary person [of same age/level of maturity] to lose self-control to the extent of intending to kill or inflict grievous bodily harm on the deceased.

Note that that conduct does not have to be performed immediately before the homicide, nor may self-induced intoxication be taken into account.

Once this defence is raised by the evidence, the onus then lies on the prosecution to attempt to rebut it beyond all reasonable doubt.

As a final point, obviously the accused may not rely on this defence if he himself had incited the conduct that then provoked him to kill the deceased.

---

[138] *R v Falconer* (1990) 171 CLR 30, 53.
[139] *R v Tolson* (1889) 23 QBD 168, 187.
[140] *Crimes Act 1900* (NSW) s 23.

Q Duress

In the long history of human misery – forcing someone else to do something they don't want to, under the threat of violence to themselves or those they love, is too common an exemplar.

The defence has two (some judgments and textbooks say three – but I've simplified it) main elements. Again, once the defence is raised on the evidence, it is for the crown to rebut beyond all reasonable doubt:[141]

(a) The otherwise criminal acts were performed under threat of violence to themselves or someone they loved/someone they were responsible for, AND,

(b) An ordinary person, in the position of the accused (and of the same age/gender) would have succumbed to the threats.[142]

R Necessity

My favourite defence. It is a perfect illustration of the recognition of two things which I hold very dear to me.

(a) Frailty: It recognises human frailty as a fundamental and inseparable part of the human condition.

(b) Non-Universality: It recognises that there are some instances where the law cannot and should not intervene. That sometimes all the best legislators and all the best judges in the world cannot create a legal system that encompasses every permutation of events. Sometimes human beings need to make tough and *impossible* decisions for the betterment of themselves and/or those that they love.

The three elements of the defence are:[143]

(a) The crime was *reasonably* believed by the accused to obstruct death and/or serious harm to themselves or another, AND,

---

[141] *The King v Anna Rowan – A Pseudonym* [2024] HCA 9 [33]-[34].
[142] Ibid.
[143] *R v Cairns* [1999] 2 Crim App Rep 137.

(b) This was the cause of the crime, AND,

(c) The crime was *reasonable and proportionate* to the issue that was otherwise evaded.

An example here can be given from a very common occurrence in the emergency department. As a doctor I'm often told stories from patients of how they raced to the hospital to ensure they received medical treatment, in time, for themselves or their loved ones. Almost always, it's a parent divulging that they were speeding down the freeway with a sick child in tow. Any parent knows they will do absolutely anything to protect their child. The law, thankfully, allows for very human responses, such as to sick children, to be protected from criminal sanction.

Again, it is for the jury to decide this. Once raised on the evidence, the prosecution can attempt to rebut it beyond all reasonable doubt.[144]

S *Sentencing*

I feel we have covered sufficient ground in both offences and defences to move on to sentencing for the purposes of this introductory book. Please note this is not a full list of all the crimes within the jurisdiction. There are many, many more. Should you be interested in looking at more crimes and/or defences – I would suggest buying a bona fide legal textbook and going nuts on it. I know I certainly did (and still do). Even law school and its dedicated (approximately) one year on this area doesn't cover everything in criminal law (as there is simply too much ground to go over).

Sentencing is the area of the criminal law with which I have the biggest personal interest. Go on any social media platform and find the nearest news article on a crime. Now go to the comments section. Invariably there will be a massive storm of comments on both sides (advocating for harsher versus more lenient sentencing) by individuals with absolutely no idea about the current regime. This is annoying.

To oversimplify, there is a massive list of both aggravating and mitigating factors (within legislation) which either increase or decrease the sentence – towards or away from the maximum for that particular crime.[145] Examples here can be given on both sides. For example,

---

[144] Ibid.
[145] *Crimes (Sentencing Procedure) Act 1999* (NSW) s 21A.

a relatively youthful offender (hence increasing chance of reform) is usually a mitigating factor. This is against something like the victim being a child (an aggravating factor) to an adult perpetrator.

Just note the purposes of the sentencing process are set out within the same legislation referenced above – these being punishment, deterrence, community protection, rehabilitation, making the offender accountable for their actions, to denounce the conduct, and in the recognition of harm to the victim and wider community.[146]

Also note the existence of many forms of sentence which may be imposed. Everything from effectively (or conditionally) 'getting off' under a 'section 10,'[147] good behaviour bonds,[148] community service,[149] fines,[150] an intervention program,[151] and all the way to a custodial sentence. The latter is a last resort, and so it should be – we in a democracy value liberty and freedom. Taking this away requires (and should require) a very high bar to be met. It's also pretty expensive (like really damned expensive); both through the cost of housing these individuals and also in taking away their ability to work and hence earn taxable money (indirectly costing money now and in the future).

Within the sentencing process, the judge (not the jury) is responsible for the formulation. There are two divergent mechanisms by which courts have been split on this issue; the two-tiered method as opposed to what is known as instinctive synthesis (I've seen it called both instinctive/intuitive in various textbooks and articles – though in class it was always referred to as intuitive synthesis). After a series of court decisions, back-and-forth on the issue, the two-tiered scheme was firmly rejected[152] and instinctive syntheses endorsed.[153] The instinctive synthesis method requires the court to both examine and assess the importance of both the subjective (external factors such as the offender's age, character etc) and objective factors (the crime itself) in one step.[154] The issue with what I've just written is that a whole bunch of decisions (both before and after) the High Court 'definitively' decided this issue have *essentially* been using the two-tiered approach – particularly in my home state of NSW. This

---

[146] Ibid s 3A.
[147] Ibid ss 10-10A.
[148] Ibid s 9.
[149] Ibid s 8.
[150] Ibid ss 14-7.
[151] Ibid s 11.
[152] *Wong v The Queen* (2001) 207 CLR 584 [74].
[153] Ibid [76].
[154] *Markarian v The Queen* (2005) 228 CLR 357 [51].

was something noticed and explicitly mentioned by the New South Wales Court of Appeal in the judgment of *Whyte*.[155] What I think we can say with some degree of certainty, however, is that the instinctive approach is *preferred* by the High Court, at this stage, and that judgments using any other formulation need to be careful in not straying too far away from its core requirements.

Naturally, with the synthesis model requiring a less formulaic process when compared to the two-tiered method, claims of inconsistency have plagued the scheme by its critics. What I would submit here, in response, is that the two-tiered method only gives the illusion of consistency. Should courts begin to place a greater weight on objective (as opposed to the subjective) factors, there would invariably be a greater degree of regularity between matters with which the objective factors of the case are similar. Yet through the lens of the (no less important) subjective factors – perhaps wildly different sentences would be present. To my mind, such a scheme could morph into a lessor form of mandatory minimum sentence structure, whereby, through subconscious bias, the sentencing judge gives too much emphasis on the crime itself and lessor regard being given to other (but by no means less relevant) issues. Strengthening this argument is the court mandating that legal principle, and consistency of legal principle, should be sought above some more simplistic mathematical equivalence of sentences.[156]

---

[155] *R v Whyte* [2002] NSWCCA 343 [157]-[159].
[156] *Hili v The Queen* (2010) 242 CLR 520 [18].

VI CONTRACT LAW

Contract law enables individuals and/or organisations to create binding legal obligations towards one another. It forms the basis of the entire economy, as without the certainty that having enforceable deals provides, who would risk trusting the word of another?

The following section will attempt to detail the basics of contract law in Australia – the making of contracts, their interpretation, their breach, and the remedies for such breaches.

A *Making a Contract*

There are five components of a valid and enforceable contract: offer, acceptance, consideration, intention to form legal relations, and certainty (various species of certainty).

1 Offer

Valid offers consist of:

(a) *Outwardly Manifested Intent:* Whether the offer would objectively be regarded as a proposal to form legal relations. Put another way, it must appear to the reasonable and sensible businessman (the standard to be used) that the offer is a bona fide proposal to form a legal contract.[157] Probably the most well-known case to law students (and was discussed in class as the paradigm example of this doctrine when I was in law school) is that of *Carlill*.[158] The case is obviously of its time – the company here was essentially selling snake-oil. Basically, they were flogging a product which they claimed prevented influenza and they also claimed that they would pay an amount of money to anyone who used their product and nevertheless caught the flu. Predictably, someone used the product and caught the flu – they then sued to get the money once the company refused to pay them. The court was very clear that it did not matter what the company (i.e. its

---

[157] *RTS Flexible Systems Ltd v Molkerei Alois Muller GmbH & Co KG* [2010] UKSC 14 [45]-[50].
[158] *Carlill v Carbolic Smoke Ball Co* [1893] EWCA Civ 1 (Lindley LJ).

directors) was actually thinking at the time they made the offer – merely that it could *objectively* be viewed as legitimate.

(b) Finality: The offer must also make clear (objectively clear - i.e. clear to a reasonable offeree) that the offeror may be bound only by acceptance.[159] If this is not present, for example some other step being necessary to conclude the deal – then no legitimate offer has yet been made. The contrary may be shown in goods displayed on shelves within a store. The lack of finality here (a shopper can always put the goods back on the shelves until the point of purchase) showcases this as merely an invitation to treat; as opposed to an offer.[160] Again, the case cited here, *Pharmaceutical Society*,[161] will almost certainly be discussed in law school classes (as it was in mine) and may appear in final examinations (from memory I think it came up in mine).

2 Acceptance

Similar to the requirements of 'offers' above, valid acceptance will be constituted if the acceptor objectively manifests an intention to accept the offer.[162] The offer will be accepted once communicated to the offeror.

An exception to this, however, is in the 'postal rule.' The rule posits that where the circumstances suggest the offer may be accepted by mail - the offer is accepted once the letter (accepting the offer) is posted.[163] The reference I have given here is one of my favourite cases (and I strongly suggest reading it in full) in which it was decided that acceptance is still valid even if the letter *never* arrives at its destination.

There are also some newer rules for electronic communications – rules which I will not flesh out here for risk of losing this book's intended brevity. Just note for now their existence and that the rules may well be different for forms of communication that are instantaneous (versus the long timeframe of traditional mail).

---

[159] *Gibson v Manchester City Council* [1979] 1 All ER 972 (Lord Diplock).
[160] *Pharmaceutical Society of Great Britain v Boots Cash Chemists (Southern) Ltd* [1953] 1 All ER 482 (Birkett LJ).
[161] Ibid.
[162] *Toll (FGCT) Pty Ltd v Alphapharm Pty Ltd* (2004) 219 CLR 165 [35]-[47].
[163] *Household Fire and Carriage Accident Co Ltd v Grant* (1879) 4 Ex D 216 (Thesiger LJ).

Another exception here is the unilateral contract (a contract by which performance also constitutes acceptance). For example, I offer the first person to do five 'push-ups' 10 dollars; acceptance here is doing the physical activity advertised (and not 'sit-ups' as an example of something that wouldn't constitute valid acceptance). The offer therefore may only be accepted by completing the contract within the same 'defined scope' as was objectively manifested by the party that made the offer.[164]

3 Consideration

Like offer, consideration maintains two components. Consideration can be summarised as being the 'price of a promise;' effectively meaning that each party, for a promise to be enforceable,[165] must gain something from agreement. The components are:

(a) *Benefit-Detriment:* Oversimplifying the matter, the concluded bargain must give each party some form of benefit (or cause a detriment).[166] Generally within contract law, there is one 'payer,' and another 'doer.' The payer causes a detriment to themselves (by paying) but gains the benefit of whatever they were buying (be it a good or service). The 'doer' causes a detriment to themselves (via performing a service or handing over a good) but gains the benefit of money. This is the most basic example of valid consideration.

Consideration may also be valid if one promises another the benefit but doesn't necessarily perform their side of agreement immediately. For example, the payer hands over money immediately to a contractor upfront. Simply because the contractor doesn't *immediately* begin on the work (that was paid for) makes the agreement no less enforceable. A promise of payment for work will likewise be equally valid. Also note, consideration at this basic level, need not be valuable – meaning that a promise for work need not be paid by money (or promised money) of equal value to be considered valid. As an example, plumbing work worth $10,000 may have $1 as consideration, or a shoelace, or a peppercorn,[167] or whatever the other party deems acceptable. Certain

---

[164] *Carlill v Carbolic Smoke Ball Co* [1893] EWCA Civ 1 (Bowen LJ).
[165] There is an exception for promises made under seal – i.e. deeds. Deeds need not have consideration to be enforceable.
[166] Ibid (Lindley LJ).
[167] *Chappell & Co Ltd v Nestle Co Ltd* [1960] AC 87 (Lord Somervell).

types of contracts, however, need valuable consideration – although this will not be discussed further here other than to state that this is mostly in the realm of contracts for real property (i.e. for land).

(b) *Quid Pro Quo:* The consideration must also meet the 'bargain requirement' of a quid-pro-quo.[168] This means that the promises need to be made in exchange for the other. That is, the consideration must induce the other party to perform their side of agreement (less the agreement be at risk of being constructed as a gift). For example, if I offer you $50 to buy an old bike of yours, I am promising you the money in exchange for the promise of the good (in this case the bike). This will be valid. This is in opposition to a circumstance where I offer to give you $50 if you beat me in a computer game. The former is an example of something being done in exchange for something else (i.e. I am giving you money in exchange for your bike). The latter, however, is an example of me 'gifting' you a benefit that was not explicitly done in exchange for anything. If I had said, alternatively, that I will give you $50 in exchange for you practising computer games for a day – then this will be valid consideration.

My favourite sub-issue within the consideration category is that of the 'existing legal duty rule.' So, I offer you $50 to paint my driveway (something which currently needs doing in real life) and you agree. At this point we have valid consideration (you get the promise of $50 and I get the promise of a painted driveway). Halfway through the work, you say you are so tired that you can't possibly do the entire driveway and offer to take the $50 for literally half the job. I then agree to this. Can I sue you to complete the work?

Because consideration was given for the full job, you are not able to use the existing consideration as the price of the subsequent promise. Hence (leaving estoppel to one side – which will be talked about later), under contract law, I would be able to sue you to complete the remaining job.[169] There are ways to 'get-out' of this issue for you – I will speak about two of these methods.

(a) *New Consideration:* Should the parties make a new price for the change in contract terms, then all will be well, as this kills the right of enforcing the old agreement to the

---

[168] *Australian Woollen Mills v Commonwealth* (1954) 92 CLR 424.
[169] *Stylk v Myrick* (1809) 170 ER 1168.

extent of the changes (as the new 'promise' has now been paid for). So, the contractor states he is tired and unable to finish the job, he then offers to decrease the price of his work to $25, and I agree to these changes. Because we have made a new promise, with new consideration, I cannot sue you to complete the job on the original terms.

(b) *Practical-Benefit:* The case of *Williams*[170] provides another exception to the rule above. However, there are a few requirements requiring fulfillment before this exception may be used. Notwithstanding these comments, the main requirements are:

(i) One-Sided and/or Unilateral Alteration: A contract has been altered by one side. That is, one party has looked at their contractual duties and then subsequently said, 'can I do something less?' This is exampled by the failure to paint the full driveway from above. The other party then agreed.

(ii) Benefit to Allow: For the agreement to alter the terms of a contract to be considered enforceable – the benefit to the offeree (offeree meaning the party that agreed to the one sided change) must outstrip any possible benefit they may see under a remedy in contract law (i.e. suing for breach). This is the primary issue for determination here.

(iii) Not Induced by Fraud/Duress: Any agreement to change the terms of a contract, to the benefit of one of the parties, must not be agreed to under fraud (a known or reckless lie)[171] or duress (the absence of choice due to some form of threat or other unconscionability).[172] Should this be the case, the secondary agreement may be deemed void (i.e. legally there never was a subsequent agreement) or voidable.

4 Intention to form Legal Relations

This is a commonsense category to ensure no daft 'agreements' end up being enforced. The test here is effectively an objective threshold of ensuring the parties actually wanted to make a

---

[170] *Williams v Roffey Bros & Nicholls (Contractors) Ltd* [1989] EWCA Civ 5.
[171] *Derry v Peek* [1889] UKHL 1.
[172] See, e.g, *D & C Builders Ltd v Rees* [1965] 2 QB 617 (Lord Denning MR). This case was decided prior to *Williams*, but despite this, it showcases neatly the principles regarding duress and part-payment of debt.

legally enforceable agreement. If I joke to you that I will pay a billion dollars if you jump in the air, and you agree – this stops you from suing me for the amount of money I will never see.

Okay, so we have a standard regarding whether the parties intended to make their agreement legally binding – what's the issue?

Well, how do we decide this? What factors may be used in considering this? Does the fact that the parties are both businessmen make it more likely? What about agreements within a family – does that make it less likely? Can we presume certain types of agreement were more highly intended to form legal relations as opposed to others?

That is exactly what was once the case.

Previously to the leading case of *Ermogenous*,[173] there were a whole bunch of presumptions regarding whether or not the parties intended to make a contract. This judgment rather clearly did away with the use of the presumptions – in favour of a more objective test of whether the parties intended to make their agreement legally binding. The funny thing is that many subsequent cases in the lower courts still effectively ended up using the very same presumptions that were gotten rid of.

I personally don't mind their use here; it can provide an easy mechanism by which information, 'at a glance,' may be provided on the likelihood of legal relations being intended. Similarly, the rebuttable nature of these presumptions also decreases the chance of justice not being done in this area.

A great case to read and see the work of the presumptions, and their rebuttal, is that of *Simpkins*.[174] In this case, we effectively had a syndicate to a lottery. It wasn't precisely a lottery – it was a fashion competition – but it was essentially a lottery (pay a small amount of money for a ticket that gives you small odds to win a far bigger amount of money). Three parties (two of which were family members and the other being a board paying tenant) repeatedly entered into the competition together and made repeated statements that they would split any winnings. The price of the tickets was also usually shared between them (they would usually take turns in paying). Predictably, one of the parties then won the prize and refused to share the winnings. It was decided that despite there being a presumption against finding any contractual intention

---

[173] *Ermogenous v Greek Orthodox Community of SA Inc* (2002) 209 CLR 95.
[174] *Simpkins v Pays* [1955] 1 WLR 97 (Sellers J).

between the parties in this domestic context – this presumption was rebutted on the facts, and their actions, when viewed objectively, were to create a legally binding agreement.

I choose this case the read because once of my best mates and I have a similar agreement for a particular public lottery in Australia. If one of us wins – we are bound to honour our agreement.

5 Certainty

For a contract to be deemed enforceable, there must be *reasonable* certainty as to the crucial terms of the contract (e.g. who is doing what, by when, and for how much).[175] Otherwise, the courts would not be sure as to what precisely they were making legally enforceable. Also note, however, is that the courts will attempt to make the contract enforceable through picking the construction that best (and/or most easily) allows enforcement.[176] My favourite (it's the funniest) case that illustrates these rules is *The Peerless Case*.[177] A contract here was made for the transport of cotton from India (very much a case of its time) to Liverpool. The parties agreed that they were buying/selling (one was buying and the other selling) the cotton from the ship named the 'Peerless.' The problem was that there were two ships with the same name and both parties thought the contract was referring to the other. The court decided that although there is a presumption in making contracts enforceable - there was nothing in this contract to aid with this particular problem (as the contract gave no indication of which ship it was referring to). The contract was thereby deemed unenforceable due to lack of certainty.

The so-called illusory contracts fail for the same reasons.[178] Illusory contracts are those agreements whereby performance of the parties is absolutely discretionary (for example, 'I will give you $50, after you paint my driveway, if I feel like it'). Clearly the agreement here is not a contract in the traditional sense, as if one party can simply evade performance, why even bother making the thing.

---

[175] *Raffles v Wichelhaus* [1864] EWHC Exch J19.
[176] *WN Hillas & Co Ltd v Arcos Ltd* [1932] UKHL 2.
[177] *Raffles v Wichelhaus* [1864] EWHC Exch J19.
[178] *Loftus v Roberts* [1902] 18 TLR 532, 534; See, also, for a more modern application of the rule (and one that will almost certainly be in any Australian law class and curriculum – and was discussed thoroughly in mine own class) *Biotechnology Australia Pty Ltd v Pace* (1988) 15 NSWLR 130 (Kirby J).

B *Terms of a Contract*

1 *Express Terms*

So, we've made the contract, now we're going to speak about its terms.

As a preliminary, and as we noted earlier, contract law cares for the objective representations of the parties (not what is subjectively within their minds). An extension of this rule is that should you sign (or otherwise agree) to be bound by a contract, then you are agreeing to be held to your bargain. It does not therefore matter whether you have read the contract or otherwise appreciate what you have signed onto.[179] The express terms of a contract are almost needless to explain, they are they terms that are written down within the contract, in black and white.

There is somewhat of an escape route, however, in some cases. This escape may be present if the terms of the contract were not incorporated into the agreement. You, in this case, therefore, are not bound by them. The inquiry into incorporation is a simple one for our purposes here. Should the terms of the contract be attempted to be incorporated after agreement, the terms are *generally* not successfully incorporated.[180] For this analysis, one must be aware of when the contract is actually formed (see *Pharmaceutical* above).[181]

The paradigm examples (however the rule also applies to other fact patterns as well) of this issue can be found within, what I call, the 'sign' cases. A ton of cases have the individual (purported to be bound) passing a sign on the way into a venue. The sign will say something like, 'this term X binds all patrons.' The contract you eventually affix your signature to will then have a term saying, 'you are bound by the sign you just passed.' The question of whether you are bound by the term is complicated. Clearly, if you have no means of seeing the sign before you agree to the contract, you are not bound. If you passed the sign previously, as the original example has written, you may well be. The overarching inquiry is one of reasonableness, i.e. is it reasonable, in all instances, to hold you bound (as the leading case of *Interfoto*[182] suggests).

---

[179] *L'Estrange v F Graucob Ltd* [1934] 2 KB 394.
[180] *Olley v Marlborough Court Hotel* [1949] 1 KB 532 (Denning LJ).
[181] *Pharmaceutical Society Of Great Britain v Boots Cash Chemists (Southern) Ltd* [1953] 1 All ER 482 (Birkett LJ).
[182] *Interfoto Picture Library Ltd v Stiletto Visual Programmes Ltd* [1987] EWCA Civ 6 (Bingham LJ).

2 Implied Terms

There are a few ways to imply a term into a contract:

(a) *Business Efficacy:* The threshold,[183] is at its core, effectively being whether the term is necessary for the operation of the contract. This assessment is essentially one of reasonableness. '*The Moorcock*' reasonableness inquiry provides the paradigm case here.[184] Another case which illustrates the rule is that of *Lister*.[185] In this case an employee ran over his father (also an employee) while in the course of employment at a company. The fundamental question was one of negligence and who owed who money. The issue for our purposes (in contract law) is that the court deemed there is an implied term that employees will take care of their employer's property – something necessary for this employment contract to actually work.

(b) *Custom:* There is a threshold perhaps best illustrated in the case of *Nelson*[186] and subsequently then approved in Australia in multiple cases (*Con-Stan*[187] being the leading case today on this issue). These hurdles are basically that the term is widely accepted; so widely accepted that every agreement (of a similar nature) is deemed use it. If this threshold is met, it is likely that the term will be implied into the contract. This is notwithstanding the possible lacking of actual subjective knowledge of this term between the parties.

(c) *Statute:* This is the most basic mechanism. If statute says a particular term must be imported into contracts of a particular species (or all contracts); then that term is automatically imported.

(d) *Class:* A term may be incorporated into a contract (to all of them in a particular class) if it is *necessary* as a matter of *law* for all contracts of this particular type (meaning the rights of the parties will be significantly impacted detrimentally should the term not be implied).[188] In *Malik,* for example, it was deemed necessary as a matter of law that there

---

[183] *Hawkins v Clayton* (1988) 164 CLR 539, 573.
[184] (1889) LR 14 PD 64.
[185] *Lister v Romford Ice and Cold Storage Co Ltd* [1957] AC 555.
[186] *Nelson v Dahl* (1879) 12 ChD 568, 575.
[187] *Con-Stan Industries of Australia Pty Ltd v Norwich Winterthur Insurance (Australia) Ltd* (1986) 160 CLR 226.
[188] *Scally v Southern Health and Social Services Board* [1992] 1 AC 294 (Lord Bridge).

is an implied term of trust and confidence in employment contracts.[189] Please also note that these terms may be removed by an express ones.

(e) *Course of Dealings:* If you've made a contract with the same other party a million times, the terms of this contract are likely imported into subsequent agreements. This can even be even though they may not be expressly written into the new agreements. Of course, should an express term be mutually exclusive with the implied term (which would otherwise be implied into the contract) then the express term will survive and the implied will not.

*Note: The legal principle of the 'parol evidence rule' also limits what terms may be incorporated into the agreement. The rule effectively negates the legal effect of verbal agreements and negotiations (of terms) where a written contract exists to determine the whole legal relationship between the parties.[190] Certain exceptions have been found in the rule - such as fraud, duress, statute, and *sometimes* in resolving ambiguity in the contract within the construction process** (among others). The doctrine also has no impact on the operation of estoppel (or equity generally). This is another reason why it is important to note the separation of the common law and equitable jurisdictions, even to this late hour. Also note, the parties may also make a separate contract, containing the missing terms, should fresh consideration be given for it. This is known as a collateral contract[191] and is only valid (in Australian law) should the terms of the two not be mutually exclusive.[192]

**Note: The process of construction (i.e. a court trying to work out what the contract actually means) is only to be used when the terms of the contract have ambiguity from the ordinary meaning of the words (that is, the words are unclear or can have multiple meanings). I provide the full judgment of *Codelfa*,[193] which everyone should read at least once (sarcasm partly intended – it is a long read, but a useful one), from its leading jurist, to best provide clarification on the issue.

---

[189] *Malik and Mahmud v Bank of Credit and Commerce International SA* [1998] AC 20 (Lord Nicholls).
[190] *City and Westminster Properties Ltd v Mudd* [1959] Ch 129 (Harman J); *Royal Botanic Gardens and Domain Trust v South Sydney Council* (2002) 186 ALR 289 [71].
[191] *Angell v Duke* (1875) LR 10 QB 174.
[192] *Hoyt's v Spencer* (1919) 27 CLR 133, 139-148.
[193] *Codelfa Construction Pty Ltd v State Rail Authority (NSW)* (1982) 149 CLR 337 (Mason J).

C Breach

There are, broadly speaking, two types of contractual breaches. There are breaches which entitle the aggrieved party to damages and then there are the breaches which entitle the aggrieved party to both damages and termination of the contractual agreement. The latter category of breaches are known as breaches of 'conditions.' There are really three technical definitions of terms, however, conditions (entitling termination), warranties (only entitling damages), and intermediate terms (those that may fall into either camp). So that's the nomenclature out of the way; labels for the three types of term, falling into either of the two macro level categories.

Conditions are terms which go to the heart (i.e. are essential) to the legal protection offered by the agreement. That is, the aggrieved party would not have entered into the agreement unless the breached term was protected. Similarly, conditions are those terms whereby breach, when viewing the contract as a whole, would enable the aggrieved party to end the contract.[194] Even a trivial breach (causing little to no loss) entitles the aggrieved party to terminate their covenant. Most matters turning on this point will effectively come down to a construction question, regarding whether or not the term was *essential* to the contract. This is because the breach will likely be established rather easily e.g. did the party deliver the good/perform the service when specified. The parties themselves may word certain specified terms of a contract to be conditions. While this is obviously highly persuasive, it is not conclusive. Naturally, statute may also deem any term as a condition (as a matter of law).

Intermediate (also called innominate) terms are those that aren't quite conditions, yet aren't warranties either. Yes I'm aware the definition is a little (a lot) shaky. The leading case effectively spells out that the ability to terminate hinges upon the type of breach and the ramifications of it. The more serious the breach, or the consequences of it, the increased chance a termination right will arise.[195]

There is a whole bunch more analysis of the different means allowing termination in addition to breach. These being the doctrines of repudiation and delay. I've always found these do not really add that much to the discussion (although there is some detail which is necessary for practising law). The two can be summarised as following:

---

[194] *Bettini v Gye* (1876) 1 QBD 183, 187-88; *Associated Newspapers Ltd v Bancks* (1951) 83 CLR 322, 328-40.
[195] *Hong Kong Fir Shipping Co Ltd v Kawasaki Kisen Kaisha Ltd* [1962] 1 All ER 474 (Diplock LJ).

(a) Repudiation: An *objective* manifestation that the other party no longer holds themselves bound by the agreement and will not (either cannot or will not) properly perform the contract. Repudiation can be by words or conduct (in one or a series of events). Just note that there is a sub-category of repudiation known as 'anticipatory breach' which is effectively repudiation of future obligations (e.g. I will not do the thing I am contractually obligated to do in the future).

For practical (as separate from nomenclature reasons) there is no real difference between the two doctrines apart from the decreased ability for the 'willing and able' doctrine (which won't be discussed in this book apart from this section) to be a barrier for termination. The doctrine in its roughest form can be summarised that an aggrieved party must show they themselves are 'able and willing' to perform the contract before they are able to terminate the agreement (on the wrongdoer's failure).

The exception to this rule is anticipatory breach. This is because the signalling, to the innocent party, they are not fulfilling their side of the bargain may well (and is likely to) diminish the performance (through lower willpower in performing a dead agreement – dead because the other party has acted or explicitly stated they won't go through with it).[196]

(b) Time: Not performing the contract within the specified time, and, time being constructed as 'of the essence.' Basically, using the phrase above (within the contract) is a means of ensuring the contract specifies the factor of time (timely performance of the contract) being a condition of it.[197]

Just use the analysis for conditions (as above) and import the timing of contract performance as a clause. Naturally (and identical to the condition analysis above), while the parties may designate to expressly state time is 'of the essence,' this is by no means conclusive within the construction process utilised by the courts (albeit it is highly persuasive).[198]

---

[196] *Laird v Pim* (1841) 151 ER 852, 857; *Foran v Wight* (1989) 168 CLR 185.
[197] Ibid.
[198] Ibid.

D *Frustration*

Say a contract is made between two parties to deliver a shipment of goods from New York to Chile by a specified time. Once the goods set sail and the boat is in the Gulf of Mexico, a diplomatic event forces the closure of the Panama Canal (either physical closure or making its transverse illegal). As such, it becomes clear to everyone that the goods can no longer get to their destination at the contracted time. Similarly, it is not the fault of either party that the contract cannot be completed. Who should bear the loss?

The common law provides for a solution here. Where the construction of the contract showcases the parties never intended to be bound in a 'fundamentally different' situation, then the contract will not be binding at the particular point of departure from what was agreed to.[199]

What specifically makes a contract frustrated is the issue that most of these cases turn upon, that is, will some change in circumstance lead to the 'fundamental difference' required for the doctrine to operate.

The words 'fundamentally different' effectively lean towards a gut feeling test of one way or another (the law's best friend of 'reasonable' does the same thing). What I will say here, is that it's pretty hard to frustrate a contract, very hard in fact. Similarly, as a general rule, illegality of actions (some new law and/or regulation making completion of the contract illegal) are more likely to create successful *frustrations* when compared to anything else.

E *Duress, Undue Influence, and Unconscionability*

As a general rule, the law does not care about your circumstances once you sign a contract – if you sign, you're bound. There are a few exceptions, however, and in this subsection, we'll go through them in our typical rough and ready fashion.

    (a) *Duress:* As you've probably guessed by now, I'm a big fan of old, particularly English cases (in which I find the legal principles more fundamentally explained and easier to grasp at first instance). This is no exception. Duress can most easily be explained by reference to the leading case of *Universe Tankships*.[200] I love the facts here – effectively

---

[199] *British Movietonews Ltd v London and District Cinemas Ltd* [1952] AC 166, 185.
[200] *Universe Tankships Inc of Monrovia v International Transport Workers' Federation* [1982] 2 All ER 67.

a union refused to work on a company's ships until the union got what they wanted (and they had a massive list of demands). The company paid a whole bunch of money to the union and then later sued for duress. The union said they were protected by industrial relations legislation. The specifics of whether the legislation covered them (the union) is irrelevant for our analysis; what we care about here is the meaning of duress. Lord Scarman is by far the most quoted jurist in this particular matter (he's in every textbook and cited in every subsequent duress case known to man). Essentially the test may be distilled down to:

(i) *Not Really a Choice:* The pressure caused the victim to be removed of free will. That is, there was no real choice for them but to agree to the terms offered.

(ii) *Dodginess:* The pressure exerted is (in the eyes of the law) illegitimate. If I offer you a house to buy, and I offer it at so low a price that you cannot refuse; this also gives rise to the absence of choice (as assessed above) but is equally (clearly) not duress. The pressure exerted must be of such a kind the law cannot abide – such as with some significant moral dubiousness.

My absolute favourite case in this area, however, has got to be *The Medina*.[201] I sincerely thank Wikipedia for leading me to this one. The Medina was a ship carrying around 600 pilgrims and crew members to Arabia. The ship ran aground in the Red Sea and another boat (*The Timor*) came to rescue everyone. Unfortunately for the immortal soul of whoever made this decision – *The Timor* refused to save anyone until a large bribe of 4000 pounds was agreed to be paid. The court refused to enforce the payment as it was obviously induced by duress.

You aren't exactly making a free agreement when you'll probably die of thirst if you don't agree to be extorted.

(b) *Undue Influence:* Effectively that the agreeing party entered into the contract due to another's *overbearing will*. There are again two types:

---

[201] *The Medina* (1876) 2 PD 5.

(i) *Presumed:* The law presumes certain categories of relationship maintain a presumption of the above undue influence (the party may rebut the presumption, however, on the balance of probabilities).

Rebuttal occurs when this party proves the other was free of their influence in making the decision. Note that the presence of independent advice to the 'inferior' party will be highly persuasive in rebuttal. The presumed categories mirror those of fiduciary relationships, although not perfectly; including (but not limited to) parent-child, trustee-beneficiary, guardian-ward, fiancés (but not spouses for some reason), solicitor-client, doctor-patient, and religious/cult leader-follower.

My favourite case here is one dealing with the cult/religious type category. In *Allcard v Skinner*[202] the follower of some religious group gave her assets to the group and later sought redress. The leading judgment here gave distinction between an individual giving away their property, due to imprudence, as compared to this being caused by the imposition of another's will overcoming your own.[203] This was an interesting case, decided on the grounds of a presumed influence, as the relationship between the follower and the church discouraged the use of independent advice. Naturally this limited the scope for rebuttal of the presumption – something which was not successfully done in this matter.

(ii) *Actual Influence:* Exactly what it says on the tin – that there was, in fact, a relationship of influence. The burden of proof lies on the plaintiff, however, on the civil standard of the 'balance of probabilities.' Typically, the cases here will have the plaintiff in some state of vulnerability (e.g. age) and relying on the defendant, in some manner, before the property transfer occurs.

(c) *Unconscionability:* This is perhaps the most simple in principle (yet complex in practice) sub-genre of voidable agreements. To grossly oversimplify here, the wrongdoer takes advantage of a *special disability* (such as intellectual difficulty) of the plaintiff (whatever

---

[202] (1887) 36 Ch D 145.
[203] Ibid (Lindley LJ).

this happens to be). The courts may then strike down such agreements – being contrary to equitable requirements of just transactions.

The leading case of *Amadio*[204] has a bank, through its representative agents, not giving full details of the transaction to an elderly couple (who didn't speak the language well) and who were securing a loan of their son. The couple mistakenly thought their liability was limited (when it wasn't) and the bank made no move to ensure they understood properly the transaction (or the bad financial situation of their son). The contract, because of this unconscionability, was set aside and liability rescinded.

For the contract to stand, once it is found that the agreement has been made between any party and another with a special disadvantage – it is up to the non-disadvantaged party to prove that the agreement was not unconscionable (i.e. fair).[205]

F *Contingent Conditions*

I won't go into a ton of detail here, just note that it is possible (in an agreement) to have performance of a contract enforceable (or non-enforceable) by the occurrence or non-occurrence of an event. I shall give an example. Before I published my first book (now available in paperback): '*An Introduction to Contemporary Political Economics*,' I sent the manuscript to various publishers. One of them sent me a contract, and within it, there were terms regarding the timing of publication (with contingent conditions embedded within).

Performance of the contract (publication) would be mandated as of 18 months from the signing of the agreement. Should a fire occur within the publishing facilities, a war begin, among other events (which may obviously impact the ability for a book to come into existence); the timing portion of the contract would be void. Contingent conditions, therefore, allow for contracts to be drafted in such a manner that most permutations of events may be considered and negotiated by both parties (prior to them occurring). This limits the ability for foreseeable events to create liability.

---

[204] *Commercial Bank of Australia v Amadio* (1983) 151 CLR 447 [12].
[205] *O'Rorke v Bolingbroke* (1877) 2 App Cas 814, 823.

Similarly, in a time of ever-increasing complexity in commercial arrangements – contingent conditions have become correspondingly important in the drafting of commercial agreements. As such, the requirement for good lawyers to also, at least, be adequate businessmen is also strongly illustrated by this doctrine. How else is a lawyer to know which contingencies to include within the contract he is drafting if he himself does not understand the commercial realities his client is engaged within?

G *Statute*

There is now a truckload of legislation dealing with commercial contracts – particularly within the realm of consumer type transactions. There is no chance I am going through all of it here. I did it in law school and hated every second – I politely refuse to do so again within the context of a book I am choosing to write (effectively for my own pleasure).

Both the *Sale of Goods Act*,[206] along with the *Australian Consumer Law*,[207] set out the do's and don'ts of commerce in Australia. Most provisions are direct mirrors of the common law, some are slight tangents off the law to create a separate remedy seeking path (such as misleading and deceptive conduct being different to misrepresentation/fraud of the common law and equity), and others create their own cause of action. A ton of provisions go towards the rights of consumers in getting refunds, replacements, and so on. If any law student is reading this book and you haven't yet gone through the legislation – have fun.

One thing I will say is that the creation of statute in this area, their regulatory agencies (such as the Australian Competition and Consumer Commission), and their tribunals of enforcement all serve to increase the sheer volume of legal matters that are being processed within this realm. This is both a good and a bad thing. On one hand it is increasing the availability of redress in commercial agreements and on the other it is spending a god-awful sum of taxpayer resources in attempting to rectify these issues (sometimes very small matters). From a normative perspective, however, it is probably a benefit that parties which would otherwise have little access to expensive litigation have at least some avenues for remedy.

---

[206] *1923* (NSW).
[207] *Competition and Consumer Act 2010* (Cth).

H *Damages*

A contract is made between two parties, one breaches the contract, the aggrieved party now sues and wins. This party is now entitled to damages as of right. The following will deal with their calculation.

The leading case in the English legal system, regarding common law contractual damages calculation, is *Robinson v Harman.*[208] Any analysis must start here, as it provides the overarching aim of contractual damages as a remedy; that being a plaintiff will be entitled to damages putting him in the same position had the contract been performed.[209]

As a general proposition, damages allow the plaintiff to recover loss based on the benefit they expected to gain from the contract. Just note there is a limited scope on the sum recoverable, by reason of foreseeability, on the part of the defendant. Let's say you have a car business, and you sign an absolutely gold-plated contract for supply of cars. For the contract to go ahead you need something repaired (like your warehouse or something) and you make a repairing contract with a third party. Should the whatever not be repaired in time, you will lose the huge benefit you were going to gain from the first contract. You did not convey this possibility of huge loss to the repairer guy when you initially made the contract. You can see where there is going now. The repair guy doesn't repair it in time, and you lose the first, 'gold-plated,' contract. Is the second guy liable for the full loss of the first contract?

These facts were pretty much replicated, and the question answered, in the leading English case (I love old English cases as you well know by this stage) of *Hadley.*[210] Here it was held that the defendant would only be liable for a loss which was foreseeable to him. This is the loss of a species naturally existing from this type of breach, or, if the possibility of 'special' loss was communicated. Hence, in the above example, should the defendant be told about the 'gold plated' contract; they will be liable for it.

Now we've dealt with the basic principle, that damages seek to put the plaintiff back in the position they would have been in had the contract been performed. Similarly, the quantum of damages only being by reference to foreseeable loss. There are two methods for this to occur:

---

[208] (1848) 1 Ex Rep 850.
[209] Ibid 855.
[210] *Hadley v Baxendale* (1854) 156 ER 145 (Alderson B).

(a) Difference in Value Damages: Let's say you order a contractor to build you a porch. You want, and pay for, a porch that increases the value of the house by $50,000. By some technical (he uses some slightly less expensive timber or something) breach, the porch only adds $40,000. This method of damages is calculable based off the value of what you bargained for, less what you got.[211] Here damages would be $10,000. These damages are to be used where the breach is slight, and the other calculation method (below), would cause an unreasonable sum to be paid to the plaintiff. There is some suggestion (in the vibes more than anything else), within the caselaw, that this line of country overlaps (however slight) with some form of unjust enrichment.

(b) 'Totally Fix the Problem' Damages: Let's use our contractor example again. Instead of a technical breach leading to a $10,000 loss; the porch is so badly built that it wrecks half the roof (causing unsafety to residents). A large portion of the house needs to be torn down, the house fixed, and then the porch properly built. In these circumstances, damages are to be calculated based off what it would take to fix the entirety of what the breach caused. This is the loss based on your reliance of the contract (plus whatever was promised). My favourite judicial (Canadian in this case) comment in these types of cases is that the plaintiff is entitled to damages to get the thing he contracted for.[212] I like it because the learned judge is basically saying, 'fix the damn house.'

(c) I Bought all this Stuff Damages: Say we make a contract for you to 'fix-up' and then mine an abandoned gold mine in a particular location. I make promises regarding the mine's location and promise you the lion's share of the profits from the resale. I'll get the minority share since you are undertaking all of the risk. You buy building materials and hire a crew. As it turns out – there is no mine in the promised location and you've wasted all this money on materials, a crew, and a whole bunch of imperishable food stuffs. You're now livid. But what exactly have you lost? You can't exactly sue for the profits of a mine never existed – that would be impossible for the court to calculate. On the other hand, we can easily count the amount of money you wasted in preparing for your side of the deal. So, in these sorts of cases, damages are calculated by reference to what you spent in fulfilling your side of the bargain.

---

[211] *Radford v De Froberville* [1977] 1 WLR 1262, 1270.
[212] *Allen v Pierce* (1895) 3 Terr LR 319, 323 (Wetmore J).

*Note: There are some cases where the plaintiff has not necessarily lost anything definite, merely a shot/chance/probability at getting a benefit. So let's say now that you wish to put a bet in a raffle. You need to be driven to the place where the raffle is being held to buy a ticket. You hire a taxi and explain this to the cab driver. The contract is to get you, from your house, to where the raffle is being held - by the betting deadline. The raffle (prize) is for $100 and there are (should you be in it) 10 hopefuls. You don't make it in time. What is your loss? Clearly it's not the full $100 as you had only a one in ten chance. The obvious answer, here, is the correct answer. Damages are generally calculated, as a rule, by reference to the chance you had in winning the whole. In this case you would get $10 - in accordance with the leading English case.[213]

This doctrine even applies where damages are not able to be measured precisely or by a matter of mathematical calculation. For example, in *Richardson v Mellish*,[214] breach of a contract meant that the captain of a ship (of the 'Honourable' East India Company – definitely a case of its time) was deprived of his captaincy. He claimed for damages for the loss of profits from two voyages despite the fact that he was only contracted for one and that the company technically would technically revisit the decision of captaincy for each voyage. He was successful in his claim for two voyages, however, because the renewal of captaincy to the same man was 'almost certain' - as the company had a practice of simply using the same captain again and again.

Granted, while calculation may be very hard in certain instances, and hence loss may be hard to prove on the facts, that does not stop the availability of damages as a matter of law (as the courts are pragmatic regarding the calculus for damages and the difficulty of sometimes assessing the exact quantum).[215]

I *Causation & Other Doctrines*

There are some limits that may reduce or remove the ability for the plaintiff to receive damages. Two of which I deal with below:

---

[213] *Chaplin v Hicks* [1911] 2 KB 786, 797-801.
[214] *Richardson v Mellish* (1824) 2 Bing 229, 239.
[215] *Fink v Fink* (1946) 74 CLR 127 (Dixon and McTiernan JJ).

(a) Causation: Similar to the law of murder we assessed previously, causation in contract law is the legal inquiry into whether the defendant, through their wrong, has actually caused the loss suffered.

I'll give an obvious example of the alternative, you get a taxi driver to take you somewhere, you are very specific in making time 'of the essence.' Due to some contractual breach, you end up not being there at the correct time and are late. You open the door and step outside of the car. At this moment, a rock drops from a height, striking you (and doing some nasty damage). You sue the taxi driver for the loss. Your argument is quite simple - if you had gotten to the destination on time, you wouldn't have been hit by the rock. To answer this question in the affirmative, being able to recover damages from the driver will require the *but for* method of causation to be applicable. This method holds that the loss would not have occurred *but for* the defendant incorrectly performing the contract. This test is accepted in Australian law as a type of preliminary hearing, namely that as a general rule, there can be no imposition of liability should the *but for* test not be met.

This being said, the test (for rather obvious reasons) is not satisfactory if used exclusively. In a world purely of *but for* causation - taxi drivers will be liable for rock throwing of others, financial advisors liable for market events out of their control, and all sorts of other ridiculous impositions of liability would be present. The test of causation, therefore, has been moulded (within contract law) to be the *but for* test; with the addition of 'common sense' causation as well.[216] That is, the loss must meet the thresholds of the *but for* test, and also, of commonsense causation as well.

In *York Montague*[217] the judgment gave an example of a doctor telling a patient that his knee was of sufficient quality to climb a mountain. The knee was, in reality, in a poor state. The patient uses this advice and moves to climb a mountain. Had he received different medical advice - he would not have done so. Unfortunately for the patient, he suffers an injury on the mountainside that had nothing to do with the quality of his knee.

---

[216] *South Australia Asset Management Corp v York Montague Ltd* [1997] AC 191(Lord Hoffman); See, also, *March v E & MH Stramare Pty Ltd* (1991) 171 CLR 506, 515 (for the application of commonsense causation in tort law).
[217] Ibid.

Should the doctor be liable? The *but for* test of causation would say yes – *but for* the shoddy medical examination the patient would not have been scaling the mountain when the injury occurred. Obviously, however, such a conclusion defies common sense – as the knee had nothing to do with the injury suffered. To avoid situations like this (and my taxi example from above) is why the test for causation must satisfy both limbs.

(b) *Mitigation:* Among other principles which limit liability, if the plaintiff could have acted in a manner which would have restrained the loss; this is generally not recoverable to the extent to which their actions have expanded (or permitted) the loss. This doctrine does not extend, however, to situations in which the plaintiff had no other option but to leave their loss unmitigated.

J *Other Types of Damages*

1 *Penalties*

Sometimes a contract will designate a price for breach – so that non or incorrect performance will automatically result in a charge of a specified amount (as payable) to the aggrieved party. I'll give an example; you hire a DVD for a week. Every day the movie is not returned post the week - you must pay $5. The benefits of this are obvious, providing a disincentive towards the breach of contract terms and also in simplifying the dispute resolution process.

What happens, however, if the contract you signed had stated the amount payable was something absurd? Let's say a thousand dollars per day. There are two paths the law can take here; either it allows any size penalty (as the parties have agreed to it), or a reasonableness test of one type or another is imposed by the courts. For fairness reasons, the courts have taken the latter approach. The doctrine was initially formulated within the leading English case of *Dunlop*,[218] where the general precedent developed so that the clause will not be judged as void (unconscionability rules apply here) if:[219]

(a) *The Sum:* The amount payable isn't of an unconscionable (daft) amount.

---

[218] *Dunlop Pneumatic Tyre Co Ltd v New Garage & Motor Co Ltd* [1915] AC 79.
[219] Ibid (Lord Dunedin).

(b) *Overpayment Rule:* In cases where the non-performed contract was to pay money; the sum cannot be larger than the amount of money which should have been made (plus interest). So, let's say the contract was for you to buy the laptop I am currently typing on for a price of $500. You obviously don't pay me. I can't charge you more than the $500 owed, plus interest, for delay in time.

(c) *Estimate:* It is perfectly okay to make the specified amount to be a legitimate estimate of the loss you will experience form non-performance. Going back to our DVD example; if on every day your store doesn't have a DVD available for hire, you will lose on average $10 - you can damn well charge me $10 for every day I don't return the thing.

2 *Loss of Bargain Damages*

Say you buy something, it can be anything, and the thing you buy is not really yours (as someone else has a better title) after the purchase. What has your consideration really bought you? Nothing.

This is known as a total failure of consideration. Whereby in effect, the price you paid for the promise has not bought you anything. In these circumstances, you can sue for the *price* of the contract (not damages).[220]

My favourite case however, just due to the sheer laughability of the facts, has got to *Rowland*.[221] In this case the plaintiff bought a car and was using it for a while. What was the issue here? Well, as it turns out, the car was stolen, and the true owner was wanting it back. As such, the buyer of the car, who had no idea he was paying money for something that was not the sellers to sell, did not actually get *anything* for his money. Hence, he was entitled to the price of the contract.

Just note that this doctrine only operates should you get *nothing* for the consideration you gave to enter into the contract. So, if you contract for someone to paint your fence, and they paint

---

[220] *Goss v Chilcott* [1996] AC 788.
[221] *Rowland v Divall* [1923] 2 KB 500 (Atkin LJ).

half of it; you cannot get the contract price, as you received *more than nothing* of the promise that was purchased.

3 *Quantum Meruit*

A contract is made between two parties to do some work. The work done is slightly different to the work that was contracted for. Maybe some work was done on top of what was contracted. Maybe the contract wasn't made properly (void) or has been terminated. Maybe a price was never specified. Maybe the contract wasn't made before the work was started and/or finished.

Effectively some work was done, the price of which the contract never stated, or the contract was not (or was never) enforceable. Crucially, the work is performed with the knowledge and acquiescence of the other party. So, for example, we make a contract that you paint my driveway a particular shade of blue and I watch you throughout the day paint it a slightly different colour than what we agreed on. Clearly, it would be quite unfair to you if I could 'get out' of paying you anything simply because the contract wasn't *technically* being performed properly. It would be different, however, if I wasn't watching you (and thereby didn't let you continue despite knowing about your screw up).

This doctrine, therefore, allows the individual who did the work to get fair payment in certain circumstances (namely consent of some type, from the other party, to do this work). Fair in this context, meaning a reasonable payment, for the work done.[222] Please also note that the starting point for reasonable payment is that of market price.[223]

K *Agency*

One of the most important sets of legal doctrine in contracts is the law of agency. It is so important because almost everyone has acted as an agent at one point in their life, and if not, absolutely everyone has acted with an agent. Agency simply refers to an individual having the ability to legally bind another. It can be in obvious situations such as in the hiring of a broker, to buy or sell something for you, or even more clearly with a power of attorney.

---

[222] *Way v Latilla* [1937] 3 All ER 759 (Lord Atkin).
[223] *Benedetti v Sawiris* [2014] AC 938 (Lord Clarke).

Agency relationships also exist in less immediately intuitive situations such as in the buying of an article of clothing from a store. Unless the transaction is conducted directly with the owner, you are dealing with an employee (an agent) who has the power to bind the shop to transactions he or she makes.

All the textbooks will refer to the new Australian cases on the subject. They are long, boring, and to be honest; they don't really enlighten you of very much. The only two cases you'll ever need (unless you are a practising lawyer) on the subject (to gain a basic understanding) are the two reasonably old English cases of *Hely-Hutchinson*[224] and *Freeman*.[225] A quick note – authority means the ability to bind the principal (that is, having authority means you have the ability to act as an agent).

> (a) *Express Actual Authority:* Firstly, actual authority is a relationship whereby the parties (principal and agent) have mutually created an agreement whereby one party may act for another. The scope of which is determined according to an inquiry of construction into the type of agreement the parties have so entered.[226] So, for example, if we agree you shall be my broker for company shares, you can't sell my house. Express authority refers to a situation whereby the (actual) authority is created by the express words of the parties involved within the creation of such authority.[227] So, if I expressly tell you that you have the right to buy and sell shares for me, you have the express actual authority to do just that.
>
> (b) *Implied Actual Authority:* This is a scenario in which the actual authority is conveyed by reason of conduct and/or the circumstances of the particular matter. It can also be created through the promotion of someone to some particular office (it is implied that they maintain the ordinary abilities of someone of that office).[228] So if I make you my stockbroker, and give you no express wording on what your rights are, you have the implied actual authority to do whatever a normal stockbroker is able to do.
>
> (c) *Ostensible Authority:* Whenever you see the words 'apparent authority' in some of the older (particularly English) cases on this matter (including the ones I am providing as

---

[224] *Hely-Hutchinson v Brayhead Ltd* [1967] 1 QB 549.
[225] *Freeman and Lockyer v Buckhurst Park Properties (Mangal) Ltd* [1964] 2 QB 480.
[226] Ibid (Diplock LJ).
[227] *Hely-Hutchinson v Brayhead Ltd* [1967] 1 QB 549 (Lord Denning MR).
[228] Ibid.

references); they are referring to ostensible authority. Ostensible authority acts basically as an estoppel (which will be spoken about below).

The doctrine prevents the principal from denying that they are legally bound to a third party, post the agent creating such an arrangement. The circumstances in which ostensible authority can be created are varied - generally requiring a representation by the principal to the third party (either directly or to the world at large) regarding the agent's authority. This is despite the non-existence of such authority *actually* existing.[229] The same can also arise when actual authority is conveyed, but also limited in some way, that the third party is not aware of.

So, as an example, I make you my stockbroker and advertise you (to the world) as such. I also state to you (and only you) that you cannot buy bank shares (for whatever reason). You, of course, then proceed to buy bank shares. I am nonetheless bound by your agreement with whomever sold the shares to you - unless the third party was aware of this limitation.[230]

Some readers here may be feeling as if this leaves the principal in an unfair position. Yes, it is true that it's pretty unfair that they will be bound by contracts that they specifically told the agent they had no authority to enter. Notwithstanding the above comments, the principal in these circumstances has the right to (and will almost certainly) sue the living daylights out of the agent which has acted beyond their authority. This cause of action against the agent somewhat mitigates the unfairness towards the principal vis-à-vis their obligations to the third party.

---

[229] *Freeman and Lockyer v Buckhurst Park Properties (Mangal) Ltd* [1964] 2 QB 480.
[230] *Hely-Hutchinson v Brayhead Ltd* [1967] 1 QB 549 (Lord Denning MR).

VII EQUITY

As we've seen, the law of contracts can be quite harsh. Should you make an agreement (objectively), the law will hold you to it, despite the possibility of (perhaps) decent reasons otherwise.

Continuing with this reasoning, the common law can generally be regarded as the simple imposition of capitalism, namely that individuals should seek to further their own interests exclusively, above the interests of their neighbours. In certain instances, however, this may not be the most desired framework. Certain types of transactions, for example, require specified professions to be mindful of their client's interests above their own. For example, do you really want your doctor to get a bag of cash for prescribing you a certain drug over another?

Similarly, there are other permutations in which the straightforward application of the common law may not be so beneficial. This section will go through a few instances in which the separate jurisdiction of equity blunts the otherwise harsh and biting edge of the common law. Just note now that while the common law will give the theoretical availability of the remedy as of right, once the case is proven, the remedies available in equity are discretionary (by reference to established doctrine). Also, the below list is by no means conclusive, again this book serves as an introduction to law, rather than a tome on every available permutation of both fact and doctrine.

A *Equitable Estoppel*

This element of equity holds that certain promises, made otherwise than by contract, can be enforceable in specific instances. I'll give two examples of promises that may be enforceable. First, let's say we make an agreement (that is for whatever reason not contractual) that in exchange for me doing some work around your estate, I will gain a portion of that estate as mine. This agreement can be summarised to be a, 'I will work for your land,' type agreement (there are a million cases of this kind in the textbooks). Another example is a situation whereby we have an existing contract for supply of something (let's say chairs). I make a few late deliveries. We then agree that you won't sue me for damages. I rely on this promise you've made me, and you sue me anyway. This latter example is in the, 'we agreed that you wouldn't enforce your rights on me,' type of case (there are also a million of these floating around).

The traditional distinction between the two types of cases has probably been removed by the leading Australian case of *Waltons*.[231] The case also provides precedent for the required factors of making out an estoppel. Please also note that different jurists within the case came to different conclusions regarding the elements needing satisfaction, and that similarly, the doctrine is not fully settled in Anglo-Australian law. The facts of this case were that a large retail company was in the process of negotiating a contract with a smaller family business (to lease some land). The negotiations were essentially finished but a final contract was not yet signed. One of the requirements of the deal was that the family would need to do a whole bunch of work on the land within strict time requirements. The family did so and met these requirements (spending a large sum of money in doing so). After all this was performed – the larger company then backed out of the deal before a contract was finalised. The family sued. The fundamental question was could they get a remedy despite there not being a finalised contract?

My personal favourite judgment, outlining when non-contractual deals would be held as enforceable by the equitable doctrine of estoppel, is as follows.[232]

> *(a) Presumptions:* The plaintiff presumed that a legal relationship existed (or will exist – such as a contract will be made) between the parties. Please also note that the assumption on the part of the plaintiff need be reasonable, meaning unreasonable assumptions will not be enforced.[233] Most other textbooks have this requirement that the assumption be reasonable as a separate point. For whatever reason, I've always found it more useful to think about it in a single step. Similarly, the inclusion of reasonableness helps in cleansing come of the criticisms towards this doctrine in removing the requirements of contract law. Namely that simply because the specific formalities of contract have not been made out, most commonly consideration, the objective reasonableness of the presumptions aids in justifying why these types of promises should nevertheless be considered enforceable.

---

[231] *Waltons Stores (Interstate) Ltd v Maher* (1988) 164 CLR 387, 404.
[232] Ibid 428-9 (Brennan J).
[233] *Western Australian Insurance Company Ltd v Dayton* (1924) 35 CLR 355, 374-5.

(b) *Defendant Causes the Presumption:* This belief held by the plaintiff was caused and/or induced by the defendant's own actions towards the plaintiff. This may occur through words or conduct and most typically occurs through the actions of the defendant's agents.

(c) *Reliance to his Detriment:* The plaintiff must rely, to their detriment, on the promise that was given by the defendant. So, in our 'work for land' case, the reliance to my own detriment would be me working on the assumption I would get some land. In the case where you promise me not to sue, for my late delivery of chairs, reliance could be in not saving money to pay you for late delivery. The reliance must also be reasonable. For example, loss from me making a contract to buy something extravagantly expensive, to be placed on the land (in our work for land case), will probably not be recoverable.

(d) *Moral Obloquy:* The non-compliance (with the agreement made) must also be unconscionable. Usually this is by reference to (and fulfilled simply by) not fulfilling what is agreed upon (which causes harm). That is, it is unconscionable to not keep your word and causing someone damage.

Just note, this category is not within this judgment, yet it is within that of other jurists within the same case.[234] Personally, I find unconscionability as necessary to justify having a doctrine of maintaining agreements outside of contract law. In my mind, the main thread within equitable estoppel, holding non-contractual agreements as enforceable, is some central point of unconscionability in not holding them as such. This is the entire reason that the law of equity exists – to aid in blunting the sharp edge of the common law with respect to moral and/or ethical considerations that the law of contracts will not, by itself, address.

---

[234] *Waltons Stores (Interstate) Ltd v Maher* (1988) 164 CLR 387 (Wilson J and Mason CJ).

B *Equitable Rescission*

Rescission is a remedy used to reverse the state of the parties to their pre-contractual position. The seller gets back the good they sold, and the buyer regains their money. There is a large distinction here between the common law and equitable rules. Under the common law, rescission is available for certain types of consideration failures such as fraud (meaning a false statement that was either knowingly or recklessly made).[235] Similarly, common law rescission is only possible should it be possible to *exactly* place the parties back into their pre-contractual positions – so called *restitution in integrum*. Should you not be able to do this for whatever reason (as alterations may have been made to what you were given, as an example) rescission under the common law is impossible.[236]

Rescission under equity is available in a broader fashion – being by reference to whether it is possible for the court to 'substantially' bring the parties back to their pre-contractual positions.[237] Should this be possible; rescission may well be available.

The remedy is possible in multiple instances within equity:

(a) *Innocent Misrep:* Firstly, we have rescission available for innocent misrepresentations. These are effectively 'lies' told before the contract was made. That being said, these 'lies' were not, however, known to be false (and not recklessly made). They do not, therefore, fall under the common law definition of fraud.

The person making the lie was honest, but perhaps a little bit stupid. If they had done some 'digging,' they most likely would have been able to find out the real 'state of affairs' of whatever they were promising.

This is what I call the 'Pippin' doctrine.

My favourite leading English case under this doctrine (*Redgrave*)[238] has the plaintiff buying a business from the defendant. The defendant makes false (exaggerated) claims regarding the income of the business. There was no evidence of these claims being made knowingly or recklessly.[239] Similarly, both the representor and the representee were a bit stupid – they both didn't actually check the income of the business from the

---

[235] *Derry v Peek* (1889) 14 App Cas 337 (Lord Herschell).
[236] See the approach in *Clarke v Dickson* (1858) 120 ER 463 (Erie J) against the later ruling in *Erlanger v New Sombrero Phosphate Co* (1878) 3 App Cas 1218 (Lord Blackburn).
[237] *O'Sullivan v Management Agency & Music Ltd* [1985] 3 All ER 351 (Dunn LJ).
[238] *Redgrave v Hurd* (1881) 20 Ch D 1 (Jessel MR).
[239] Ibid.

paperwork – but both had ample time to do so. Despite their equal stupidity and lack of due diligence, the court found neither was a bar for substantial rescission. The contract was therefore unwound, and the parties returned to what was effectively their pre-contractual state.

The key here, is similarly to the 'not guilty' against 'innocent' analysis from criminal law. The finding of an 'innocent' instead of a 'knowingly made' falsehood does not mean that it was not, in fact, made fraudulently. It does mean, however, that there is no evidence to support such a claim. Calling someone a fraudster is a very serious charge to levy, hence the high threshold needing to be hurdled, something I personally find very beneficial due to its seriousness.

(b) *Things we've already talked about:* Earlier in this book we spoke about contracts which may be judged as void due to duress, undue influence, and unconscionability. This remedy may also be used to reverse the perverse impacts felt by agreements made within these categories. Again, substantial restitution must be possible for this to occur. Similarly, the other bars to equitable relief (such as not having unclean hands – discussed in later sections of this book) must also be met.

(c) *Things we're soon going to talk about:* Later in this book we're going to speak about fiduciary relationships and trust law. Transactions, be they contractual or not, made in breach of these equitable precepts, may also be voidable (giving rise to the possibility of rescission).

C *Fiduciary Relationships*

As already mentioned, at common law, one only has the responsibility to stay within the bounds of legality - yet otherwise can pursue purely selfish aims. The law of fiduciary relationships ensures that certain categories of transaction have parties that maintain a deeper level of duty towards others within the same transaction or series of transactions. Sometimes they flow solely in one direction. So, a lawyer owes a duty to the client but not necessarily the other way around. Other times the duty is mutual, for example partners in a business owe the duty to one another. In identifying when these relationships arise, one must be aware of two overlaying doctrines:

1. *Presumed as Fiduciary:* There are a whole list of relationships, in which the leading Australian case of *Hospital Products*[240] goes through, whereby fiduciary relationships are presumed as a matter of law. These being the partner-partner (in a business partnership), lawyer-client, trustee-beneficiary, agent-principal, director-company, servant-master, and tenant for life-remainderman. Important to note here is that this list is by no means closed and new presumed relationships may arise in the future.

2. *Factual:* Where the relationship is not part of the above list, the plaintiff may prove the relationship was of the fiduciary species. Interesting to note, here, is that there is no sole accepted test within the Australian authorities for determining whether a relationship has a fiduciary quality. There are two leading cases at the same level in the court hierarchy (both at High Court level). Hence it is important to examine both of them before coming to any conclusion.

> *(a) Undertaken to act as Fiduciary:* Again, in *Hospital Products,* we see Justice Mason outline the famous 'undertaking' principle - whereby a fiduciary relationship exists where one party agrees to 'act for or on behalf of or in the interests of another.'[241] This seems to be the test most widely accepted in England as well.[242] My favourite illustration (for its simplicity) of this rule is in *Nottingham;*[243] whereby an employee may only be deemed to be in a position, as fiduciary for their employer, should the agreement showcase such a requirement.

> *(b) Indicia:* The second leading Australian case on this matter is *Breen;*[244] whereby the court lists a bunch of indicia (not conclusive factors) which may indicate the existence of the fiduciary relationship:[245]

---

[240] *Hospital Products Ltd v United States Surgical Corporation* (1984) 156 CLR 41, 68.
[241] Ibid 96-7 (Mason J).
[242] *Bristol and West Building Society v Mothew* [1998] Ch 1 (Millet LJ); *Henderson v Merrett Syndicates Ltd* [1995] 2 AC 145, 205 (Lord Browne-Wilkinson).
[243] *Nottingham University v Fishel* [2000] EWHC 221 (QB) (Elias J).
[244] *Breen v Williams* (1996) 186 CLR 71.
[245] Ibid 107.

(i) *Confidence:* Should the proposed beneficiary of such a relationship have a high degree of trust in the fiduciary – this will evidence the existence of such a relationship. The condition of trust being perhaps the core element of the fiduciary relationship – namely that one party may trust another to do right by them (even over themselves).

(ii) *Bargaining Power Inequality:* Should one party have an advantage in bargaining over the other – this will likewise indicate the existence of such a relationship.

What I would say here is that there are many instances, in which bargaining power may be unequal, which do not influence the existence of a fiduciary relationship. That is, *mere inequality* of bargaining position, without more, is usually insufficient.

So, for example, you are the sole manufacturer of some good that others highly demand; this fact alone does not predispose the relationship to be that of the fiduciary. What is needed is more of an imbalance of knowledge within the context of whatever the fiduciary is performing. So, for example, the relationship between a lawyer and their client being of such a kind where one party has little to no knowledge on the matters the lawyer will be pursuing, or what is required (financially) in doing such work, and so on.

(iii) *An Undertaking:* This is the 'undertaking principle' found above. Because the two cases are from the same level in the court hierarchy and the latter test does not explicitly usurp the former, it is unknown as to whether the two tests are separate, or whether this 'indicia' inquiry has overtaken the undertaking principle (and demoted it to being merely a portion of a larger examination). What I would propose is to ere on the side of caution and therefore one must look at both tests in isolation.

(iv) *Mercy:* Should the beneficiary of such a relationship be at the mercy of the decisions made by the fiduciary (such as strategic decisions of a lawyer, or diagnosis of a doctor etc), to the extent that their rights or interests may be impacted, this will likewise give strong evidence that the fiduciary relationship exists between these two (or more) parties.

Let me give an example here from my own experiences as a doctor. Many times, on a night shift, I am called to an elderly patient, suffering from dementia, who has their vital signs deranged in some way – most commonly a fever. There are no other doctors around at this time (there are, but I have to call them for assistance), the patient is non *compos mentis* and is thereby incapable of caring for themselves. The are thereby totally (and unambiguously) at the mercy of my decision making. They receive the examination I perform on them, the tests I order for them, and the treatments I give them. They will not receive any other. It is a terrifying responsibility to have another's life and wellbeing in your hands like this. Nothing can quite prepare you for it, nothing can explain it adequately, and nothing else is quite like it. The law (through equity) in these situations ensures that there are legal guardrails in place to make certain that the only things I can take into consideration, when making these decisions, is the patient's wellbeing, and that I cannot breach my fiduciary obligations when treating patients in this situation. If I may plug the profession for a moment, I am gladdened that every single other physician I have met also takes their obligations *very* seriously. I have not yet met another doctor who doesn't equally view their duty as sacred.

(v) *Reliance/Vulnerability:* Should one party be dependent on the other for whatever reason, this will likewise illustrate (and give evidence towards) the fiduciary relationship (similar to the above category, e.g. a patient depends on the doctor acting in their interests in prescribing drugs or other treatment).

3 *Scope – What Actions are Protected?:* You go to a lawyer and ask for legal advice. During the course of this (giving the legal advice) the lawyer accidentally spills his hot coffee on you –

has he breached his fiduciary duty? Obviously, the answer in this ridiculous scenario is a resounding negative.

For a fiduciary to breach their duties, they must do exactly that - breach their duties. To determine, however, what exactly their duties actually are to you in particular scenarios, you must construct the agreement between the two parties and discern what they actually agreed to do on your behalf (and to what extent your interests are placed over theirs).[246]

The lawyer here who spills his coffee on you is not liable for breach here (although the law of negligence might provide decent damages if the burns were bad enough). This is opposed to a scenario in which he purposefully gives you bad advice in circumstances where they stand to gain a financial windfall (let's say they give bad advice on your driveway painting business and the lawyer is the primary shareholder in its main competitor).

4 Breach:

Unlike our Canadian counterparts,[247] Australia follows the traditional English doctrines regarding what the fiduciary duties (and hence what breach of these duties) entail. Breaches of the fiduciary duty come in two flavours:

(a) *Unauthorised Profits:* Should a fiduciary make a profit (any profit), within their scope as fiduciary, and that profit was unauthorised, this is breach.[248]
The case of *Parker*[249] provides the clearest judgment in favour of this rule – it's just glorious. Again, Wikipedia to the rescue in providing the exact quote.
'I do not think it is necessary, but it appears to me very important, that we should concur in laying down again and again the general principle that in this Court no agent in the course of his agency, in the matter of his agency, can be allowed to make any profit without the knowledge and consent of his principal; that that rule is an inflexible rule, and must be applied inexorably by this Court, which is not entitled, in my judgment, to receive evidence, or suggestion, or argument as to whether the principal did or did not suffer any injury in fact by reason of the

---

[246] *Kelly v Copper* [1993] AC 205, 209-15 (Lord Browne-Wilkinson).
[247] *Breen v Williams* (1996) 186 CLR 71, 94-5; 112-13.
[248] *Parker v McKenna* (1874-75) LR 10 Ch App 96 (James LJ).
[249] Ibid.

dealing of the agent; for the safety of mankind requires that no agent shall be able to put his principal to the danger of such an inquiry as that.'[250]

The exact requirements (I split it into three) of an unauthorised profit are as follows:

    (i)   *Profit:* Pretty obvious what this consists of - some financial benefit (in one shape or another).

    (ii)   *Within Scope:* The profit must be made within the *scope* of the fiduciary relationship to be considered a breach.

           By way of illustration, you retain a lawyer; during the course of dealings with them they are retained by someone else on an unrelated matter and earn a profit from that unrelated matter. It would be ludicrous to make this a breach. If, however, the lawyer used the information you gave him about your matter (let's say about the miserable state of your company – and perhaps even leaked it) and with that information bought shares in your competitor (and made a windfall from it) then this will be considered breach. Even in less serious breaches whereby all parties made a profit, or some (but not all principals) agreed to the profit; the lawyer will be liable.

    (iii)   *Unauthorised:* Subject to the authorisation (consent) rules (as explained below) - the profit must not be permitted by the beneficiaries of the fiduciary relationship.

(b) *Conflict of Interest:* This category comes in two further sub-categories. Just note that the threshold of a 'possibility of breach,'[251] has been interpreted in the leading case, to mean that a reasonable man (when looking at the circumstances) would think there was a 'real sensible possibility of conflict' (and that this will constitute breach).[252] Please also note that my example of 'chair making' used throughout this book comes directly from the facts of *Aberdeen*;[253] whereby a company was engaged to make iron chairs.

---

[250] Ibid.
[251] *Aberdeen Railway Co v Blaikie Brothers* (1854) 1 Macq 461 (Lord Cranworth LC).
[252] *Boardman v Phipps* [1966] UKHL 2 (Lord UpJohn).
[253] *Aberdeen Railway Co v Blaikie Brothers* (1854) 1 Macq 461.

(i) *Conflict of Duties:* This is where the fiduciary is bound by two sets of duties – each one in competition with the other. Say your lawyer is advising you regarding your upcoming litigation with your main competitor, and unbeknownst to you, they are doing the same thing with the other party. In this circumstance the practitioner is torn between their duties of loyalty towards both parties. This is a clear example of breach in this instance. The reasoning is here pretty straightforward; should the lawyer fulfil his duty to the upmost to one party, then they will undoubtedly breach it to the other.

(ii) *Conflict to Self:* This is the more 'clear cut' example, as seen in *Boardman*.[254] A fiduciary who stands to personally gain from not acting in the best interests of another will rather clearly be breaching their obligations. Back to our lawyer example, should the lawyer not disclose to you that he has a rather large financial stake in the main competitor you are seeking advice regarding litigation on – this is clearly a breach (being in their interests to advise you wrongly). This is due to there being a 'real and sensible possibility' they will choose their own interests above yours.

5 *Consent:* The essence in a claim of breach against a fiduciary is that the principal was not aware and therefore did not consent to it. Similarly, there is also the possibility that the beneficiary *could not* have consented to the breach (examples include that the principal was a child and/or had intellectual disabilities). Should consent be established, the cause of action falls away. The rule here, is that the fiduciary's disclosure is sufficient, only if it highlights *all material matters* of conflict, along with the full range and character of what would otherwise be a breach. I'll give two illustrations from our lawyer examples (one for each species of breach) to highlight what is required.

(a) *Profit:* In the scenario in which the practitioner uses your information to purchase shares which stand to make him a profit; only full disclosure to the principal of what he intends to buy, and how much, will be sufficient. Anything less than that will not meet the high barrier of disclosure.

(b) *Conflict:* There are two possible contrivances.

---

[254] *Boardman v Phipps* [1966] UKHL 2.

(i) *Duty:* In our example in which the solicitor was giving advice to both sides of the litigation – only full disclosure to BOTH parties will be sufficient (as he owes fiduciary duties to both).

(ii) *Financial Interest:* Similar to the 'profit' category above, only revealing the full nature of your investment in your primary business competitor (in the example above) will remove you from the possibility of being found liable for breach.

Naturally, the principal must also consent to the breach, as simply stating that you are going to breach the duty, without consent from the other party, will obviously not be sufficient to remove liability.

Similarly, any actions in furtherance of another's interests (anyone bar the principal), before consent has been given, will be a breach in and of itself. Likewise, should you disclose one set of conflicts, but not another, you as fiduciary are not expunged from liability (as full disclosure is required). This may seem immediately obvious, but I remember wondering that very question; something along the lines of: 'does disclosure of one set of conflicts result in a situation whereby *all conflicts of the same character* are covered?' The answer is, unsurprisingly, a resounding no.

D *Trusts*

This is perhaps the most misunderstood and maligned area of law (apart from, and secondary only to, anything to do with criminal sentencing and criminal procedure generally). Those on the 'left' of the political spectrum will howl from the rooftops regarding the ability for trusts to minimise taxation in wealthy individuals and/or families. What I would say about this, is that while it is true trusts are not uncommonly used for that purpose – so too is debt, or depreciation techniques, and also an uncountable litany of accounting tricks too.

The funny thing about these criticisms, is that should there be proof regarding the subjective intentions of the creation of a trust, and that the property isn't really being dealt with as the trust demands, and this intent is to dodge taxes (or screw over a creditor), the trust may be made void by the court.

The problem here is not an issue of legality, meaning that as a matter of law, there is nothing theoretically stopping a trust being declared a nullity for taxation minimisation purposes. This requires that the above criteria (that the trust property is not *really* being dealt with in accordance with its terms) is met. The problem is one of evidence, however. That is, there needs to be evidence to show the trust isn't being used as was originally manifested – but instead for some other nefarious purpose.

Similarly, there are also rather compelling reasons why trusts are a useful tool within society. Say you are married and wish to write a will in favour of your kids should both you and your partner pass away. Typically, control of the estate will be passed to an adult before the child reaches majority. This adult is generally a sibling or perhaps a damn well trusted (pun intended) friend of the parents. This is a trust.

Notwithstanding the above commentary, trusts enable the property to be kept safe on behalf of the children (in this scenario), with the force of law (above simply your trust in the other person), making sure this dynamic remains stable and safe. I have a rhetorical question before I move on – how many siblings throughout history would have screwed over the kids of their dead brothers/sisters were trusts not able to safeguard the property? Arguably the greatest play ever written, *Hamlet*, deals with this very issue. This is why I get annoyed whenever I hear about some scheme by a 'populist' politician to 'crack down' (whatever that even means) on trusts.

Be careful what you wish for, you might just get it.

Moving on, the following will detail a discussion on the making of trusts.

1 *Making Trusts*

There are a few requirements needing satisfaction regarding trust creation. More requirements are needed still for birthing specified trusts as separate from those requiring simple declaration (that is, specific formalities are needed for testamentary trusts and trusts created by property transfer). These will be summarised post the general principles being dealt with. The foundation on which trust law stands, has precedent in the leading case of *Knight*,[255] whereby the 'three certainties' requirement for trust creation was established. That is what almost all the

---

[255] *Knight v Knight* (1840) 49 ER 56 (Lord Langdale MR).

textbooks say, namely that the case of *Knight*[256] was the first to outline this principle. The problem with this, however, is that a fair few cases before *Knight* say much the same thing! For example, the case of *Wright* (some twenty years – the earliest case I could find) prior to *Knight* has Earl Eldon stating that the subject (the property), the objects (the beneficiaries), and the intention to create a trust must be certain.[257] Please also note that the 'three certainties' requirements have been approved by Australian courts.[258]

Regardless of this timeline trivia - what is needed to create a trust is as follows:

    (a) Certainty of Intent: The settlor (the person making a trust) must intend to do so. The leading Australian case of *Byrnes*[259] sets out the test for certainty (of intention to make a trust) as an objective one through the approval of the English case *Twinsectra*.[260] The subjective intentions of the party creating the trust was stated, by one jurist, to be 'irrelevant.'

Similar to our analysis on the making of contracts, should the individual objectively manifest the intention, in this case for the creation of a trust, then they will be deemed to do so. This is despite their perhaps contrary subjective intentions. The objective intent, therefore, need be that the formation of a trust, as constructed by the court, is the best way to do whatever the settlor objectively manifested that they wanted to do.

    (i)   *Exceptions – Public Policy and Sham Trusts – Answering Populist Criticisms:* As I mentioned above, the so-called sham 'trust' is an exception to this doctrine (this is what was referenced earlier as the theoretical allowance of declaring a trust void as a matter of law). Most textbooks here will reference *Midland Bank*,[261] but, as always, I will reference another earlier case which I have personally found more eloquent and succinct in its definition (at least at this introductory level). The case of *Snook*[262] has the leading judgment effectively describe a 'sham trust' as being a scenario in which the documents say that some particular legal relationship (in the form of a trust) is created. However, the

---

[256] Ibid.
[257] *Wright v Atkyns* (1823) Turn & R 143 (Earl Eldon LC).
[258] See, eg, *Kauter v Hilton* (1953) 90 CLR 86, 97.
[259] *Byrnes v Kendle* (2011) 243 CLR 253, 274.
[260] *Twinsectra Ltd v Yardley* [2002] 2 AC 164, 185 (Lord Millet).
[261] *Midland Bank Plc v Wyatt* [1997] 1 BCLC 242.
[262] *Snook v London and West Riding Investments Ltd* [1967] 2 QB 786 (Diplock LJ).

actions and subjective intention of the parties say something else entirely. That is, the legal relationship created *on paper* is not followed in practice, nor perhaps is the real intent behind the creation of the legal relationship what it outwardly appears.

There also appears to be, in some later judgments (both in Australia and England), a flavour of *actual fraud* in the sham trust. Judgments in both jurisdictions have heavily implied, if not outright stated, that the sham trust is a legal device used in the *deliberate deception* of third parties.[263]

I'll give an example; a trust document is created to split the property of a family amongst its members. The document states that this is done to secure the financial security of the family so that a rash decision by one member (let's say the father, who currently owns all the property) cannot harm the long-term security of the others. The document also states that the property is to be utilised by joint vote of all members (so the above intent is affected). In reality, the father still has control of all the property, the document only truly existing to minimise taxation (as now the income from such an estate is split amongst the members of the trust according to their share; and hence they fall into lower tax brackets). This trust, should evidence be found regarding the true nature of property use, will likely be declared by the court as invalid (generally the lawsuit will be initiated by the taxation department in this type of scenario). The problem here is that there is unlikely to be an email, or SMS, or written note saying something to the effect of, 'The property is still controlled by me/dad/my husband,' as who in their right minds would be so irresponsible or act so against their own interests in such a way.

As a slight side note, such an issue has been used by many a conservative voice to be another pillar in support of a flat taxation system (something I myself have been flirting with supporting). For a full explanation of my own current views on the matter, my other book goes into significant detail. The argument follows, should there be no (or fewer) tax brackets, there would be no (or lesser) incentive to generate these 'sham' trusts as they would give no benefit (or lesser benefit) in lower taxes. Despite the

---

[263] *Raftland Pty Ltd as trustee of the Raftland Trust v Commissioner of Taxation* (2008) 238 CLR 516 [35], quoting *Hadjiloucas v Crean* [1988] 1 WLR 1006, 1019 (Mustill LJ).

contrary arguments against such taxation schemes (the upward pressure on inequality would be rather high); everyone should be able to admit this as a possible benefit.

(b) *Certainty of Subject:* The term subject refers to the property which is to be placed on trust. The law here, for lack of a better phrase; is a little weird. The general rule is that there needs to be specific property (that the trust instrument identifies) as placed on trust. I personally find the case of *Re London*[264] particularly strange whereby the learned jurist took issue with the ability for a trust to make certain that 50 bottles of wine (from a mass of identical bottles) was sufficiently certain. The judgment went on to say this wine case is analogous to 'two sheep from a larger flock' being similarly uncertain. While I would agree with the judgment regarding the sheep, as different animals have different characteristics; the analogy, at least in my mind, may be distinguished due to the same bottles of wine being sufficiently fungible to have a set amount from a mass being equal enough to a different set amount from the same mass. I would propose the bottles of wine being far more akin to money; whereby one set of $50 from a larger bank balance is the same as the next fifty. That is, one need not identify which specific dollars are to be held on trust, merely the aggregate amount. I think this is why we see such an uneasy judgment in *Re Harvard*,[265] whereby the distinction between chattels and intangibles was seen as the only mechanism in which the precedent could be reconciled. What I would instead propose is a more basic test of whether the subject proposed (to be placed on trust) is sufficiently fungible for the test of certainty to be met in situations whereby the trust instrument outlines an amount from a greater bulk instead of specific items. This could be criticised on the basis that the test could devolve into a 'gut feeling' type analysis. I may surprise you, however, in agreeing with this conclusion. Every 'reasonableness' test in law does the same thing. That is, something is reasonable if your gut tells you that it is. This would be no different. I would submit such a test regarding whether the trust property is sufficiently fungible as a better framework than the artificial (I would propose at least) separation of chattels and intangible property.

---

[264] *Re London Wine Co (Shippers) Ltd* [1986] PCC 121 (Oliver J).
[265] *Re Harvard Securities Ltd* [1997] EWHC Comm 371 (Neuberger J).

(c) *Certainty of Object:* Object here refers to certainty regarding who the beneficiaries of the trust are and what their share of trust property is. In general, there are two broad categories of trust; those where the beneficiaries and their share within the trust is fixed (family trusts generally follow this formula – e.g. the trust naming each member in a family and specifying their share of trust property) and those where the beneficiaries are a theoretical class, with the share to be determined at trustee discretion. I will say now that the adoption of the latter category was a long and drawn-out process, in Australia, with the State Supreme Courts and Federal High Court often coming to different conclusions on the matter. The current rules for the two classes are as follows:

(i) *Fixed Trusts:* As briefly described above, for a fixed trust to be sufficiently certain, each individual beneficiary need to be listed by name (beneficiaries are treated as an exclusive list and as individuals) for the purposes of this species of trust. Their share also needs to be at the same level of certainty; each member needing to have a defined interest of their share of the trust property.[266] Just note the reference given is not the most cited precedent for that particular test (coming from England) but instead my favourite (most illustrative and simple) description of the rule.

(ii) *Discretionary Trusts:* The leading case on trusts of this flavour (which frankly totally upended the law on trusts at the time of judgment) is *McPhail*.[267] The facts of the case basically had the trust instrument stating that members of some company (and their families) could access trust funds at the unilateral (ultimate) discretion of the trustee. Naturally, the challenge (since we are talking about it here) was such that the trust may not have been sufficiently certain in regards to objects – the instrument not listing names of the individual beneficiaries nor their relative share. The leading judgment here was rather scathing against the traditional doctrine and effectively re-stated the test to be one of accurately constructing the settlor's true intent. That is, should the trust identify members of a 'particular class' as being within (or without) the instrument's scope, then the trust shall not fail for uncertainty on this front.[268] We inevitably get into the

---

[266] *Federal Commissioner of Taxation v Vegners* (1989) 90 ALR 547 [12] (Gummow J).
[267] *McPhail v Doulton* (1971) AC 424.
[268] Ibid (Lord Wilberforce).

same discussion regarding the difference between theoretical issues as a matter of law and whether or not the evidence supports such a conclusion. Similar to our discussion above into the legal and factual inquiries into the so called 'sham' trusts, we have a similar discussion present here. Merely because there may be an evidentiary issue in deciding whether particular individuals happen to fall within a specified class; this does not equate to the trust instrument lacking object certainty. That is, as long as it is *theoretically* possible to determine whether (or not) a claimant lies within the specified class, the instrument is sufficiently certain of object (regardless of the difficulty in actually proving this through the evidence) to be held as valid by the courts.

The difference is as follows; between an inquiry of, 'what is this particular class?' against something like, 'are YOU a member of this class?' The former being a *theoretical inquiry* which requires satisfaction under object certainty. The latter, however, is an *evidential inquiry* irrelevant for this discussion of object certainty.

(d) Special Types of Trust: The above sections detail the general rules for the making of a trust by declaration. The two other types of trust (mentioned in this book) have their own peculiar rules which need to be satisfied before the trust is correctly made in the following circumstances. I remember dealing with this in law class and thinking to myself that surely any court of equity should be able to circumvent these formalities – I was partly right in this.

(i) *Trusts by Will:* This is pretty simple, a will is just another means to create a trust by declaration – merely the declaration is made on the will document. The requirements for this can be seen in the statement above; you need a declaration satisfying the three certainties as already described. You *also* need a will document. This will document needs to satisfy a bunch of formalities for a will to be legitimate. These are usually described in statute specific to the jurisdiction. This being said, even if this is not done correctly, it may not matter overly much, as the courts (using their equitable jurisdiction) have the ability to determine anything a valid will (if they deem it necessary to do so).

(ii) *Trusts by Assignment:* Assignment refers to the recognition, by law or equity, of a transfer of property from one person to another. So, similar to what we said directly above, we need an assignment that is recognisable either by law or equity. We also need the declaration rules (i.e. the three certainties rule) to be likewise met.

Now, for the most obvious rule in the history of the universe - the declaration that the assigned property is to be held on trust must be ***before*** the assignment. So, you can't give over your property to someone else (as a gift) and then later claim it's to be held on trust – you've got to claim it's a trust first and then hand it over. This comes up in law school exams, law school classes, and all the textbooks – it's a common-sense rule in distinguishing between transfers of property as gifts versus the creation of trusts. Remember that objective manifestations of intent are what the courts care about, not what was subjectively in the minds of the persons making the transfer.

2 Trust Duties

At this point in the analysis, every legal textbook will begin with about fifty or so pages of listing and describing every single duty a trustee maintains in their position as trustee. This office is no light affair, it is a serious position in which failure to comply with any duty may enable removal from office and open a cause of action against the trustee. Don't volunteer to be a trustee if you don't know what you're doing and/or if it's not totally necessary; it can be a tough gig. I'll now go through a few of the duties – the most important ones anyway.

(a) *The Irreducible Core:* The most important set of duties imposed on a trustee, in their administration of the trust, were developed in the landmark judgment of *Armitage*[269] (whereby this core set of duties were first articulated in their entirety). Effectively, the case outlines the following duties as irrevocable, else there will not be a trust:

(i) *Good Faith:* The trustee must perform their obligations in good faith, for the benefit of the beneficiaries, and not for any ulterior motive. An example of this may be seen in the execution of any trust power; whereby should the trustee be

---

[269] *Armitage v Nurse* [1998] Ch 241 (Millet LJ).

found to make a decision on any criteria not bounded by an overarching wish that the decision be in the best interests of the beneficiary – the trustee will likely be found liable for breach of trust. Again, we run into the same nasty trouble of actually finding evidence for something (to be proven) as being separate from the theoretical ability, at law, for the doctrine to be utilised. Should we find an email saying something like, 'I used my trust power not for the benefit of the beneficiaries,' they will be liable – despite how admittedly unlikely that is. This being said, the offending conduct may also be construed *objectively* as being not in good faith.

(ii) *Honesty:* Thou shalt not commit fraud in your dealings with the beneficiary. There is a duty to act honestly in all dealings and in exercising any duty or power imparted on the trustee via the trust instrument.

(iii) *Terms:* While this was not specifically outlined within the leading case – there is a blindingly obvious rule that the trustee should follow the trust terms. Should this duty be breached, there will be serious repercussions for the trustee. Now is where we get into dicey waters - should the trust be breached unintentionally (i.e. with negligence) then the repercussions (of which) will be very different from circumstances in which it was intentional. This will be impliedly spoken about (in later sections of the book) but just note now that an intentional breach is highly likely to overlap with the above two categories - making it so the trustee cannot be trusted to adequately perform their obligations.

(b) *Duty to Account:* Trustees are bound to keep a full record of their administration of the trust, for the eyes of the beneficiary (to justify their administration of the trust), should they wish to see it.[270] There is a whole bunch of precedent regarding what specifically the beneficiaries have the right to see (as they are not able to have access to everything having to do with the trust). For example, in a discretionary trust, the trustee may make notes for themselves regarding what they personally see as the requirements for handing out trust property. This will clearly not be for the view of the beneficiaries as they may mould their circumstances to come within the ambit of the trustee's self-imposed

---

[270] *Ultraframe (UK) Ltd v Gary Fielding & Ors* [2005] EWHC 1638 (Ch) (Lewison J).

factors (which may influence their actions under the trust). My favourite illustration of the rule here is in the case of *Bosworth*,[271] whereby the test was effectively articulated as one of a right to an account, as opposed to that information best articulated as 'secret' by the trust instrument itself (or those having anything to do with discretion).[272] Bosworth is my favourite case here for two reasons. Firstly, it is a simple articulation regarding the right to account. Secondarily, it contains the name Bosworth. For those who know me, or are generally fans of history, you've probably already guessed the reasons for my enthusiasm. Bosworth is the name of the last decisive battle in the Wars of the Roses in which the 'red rose' Henry VII of House Lancaster slew King Richard III (the 'white rose') of York - taking the throne of England and changing the fate of the world. All this despite Richard's army outnumbering Henry's. It is said that any small twist of fate can change the tide of history – this is an excellent example. Continuing with this tangent, this is one of the many reasons why I am not amongst those who criticise so-called 'great man history.' Sometimes in the course of the history of mankind, it is indeed a single person, who, almost singlehandedly, changes the direction of the tides.

(c) *Duty of Care:* The case of *Armitage*[273] had one of the parties submitting to the court that the duty to act without negligence was part of the irreducible core (meaning liability couldn't be limited or removed, for the trustee, within the instrument which creates the trust). Considering we have delved into this irreducible core earlier, this argument unsurprisingly failed. The reasoning for this failure was that English law has traditionally, and continues to, make a distinction between negligence (even severe negligence) and dishonesty (though sometimes gross negligence may be evidence of *mala fides*).[274] One can be a fool, but as long as one acts as an *honest* fool, then the law will treat you less harshly than it would a fraudster.

That being said, some of the most common breaches of trust duties involve some degree of negligence on the part of trustee within their handling of trust assets (namely in investment and other powers which will be discussed further below). To gain an introductory knowledge, one really needs to know the two cases mentioned here for a

---

[271] *Re Bosworth* (1889) 58 LJ Ch 432.
[272] *Tierney v King* [1983] 2 Qd R 580.
[273] *Armitage v Nurse* [1998] Ch 241 (Millet LJ).
[274] *Goodman v Harvey* (1836) 4 A&E 870, 876 (Lord Denman CJ).

general understanding. Both are English and one is extremely old. The first is a statement of the rule from the leading judgment of *Speight*,[275] whereby the duty of care was characterised as that of an 'ordinary and prudent businessman.' This can be distilled further to basically be defined as a *reasonable* businessman. As for another case which highlights an application of this rule, regarding liability of trustees, we turn to merry England a long time ago. So long ago that what would later become the thirteen colonies were only partly in the hands of the English. At this time, the 'New Netherlands' of the Mid-Atlantic (including New Amsterdam – which later would be re-named to New York) was in a period of flux between English and Dutch rule. At the same time within Europe, Oliver Cromwell had only recently passed away and French King Louis XIV ('The Sun King') was arguably the most powerful ruler on the face of the world. That long ago, the trust dispute of *Morley*[276] had a trustee being found not liable for a sum of gold taken/stolen (by another) from the trust account. This escape from liability was founded on the basis that the trustee had done his duty without negligence, and that therefore, no more was required of him. That is, the trustee was not negligent in his handling of the trust account, and so, no liability could be founded against him. Had the trustee been negligent in their securing of the trust account, say for example by leaving the property in plain view, the opposite finding would have been likely. The case highlights the rule that a trustee does not get punished for bad things happening to the property of the trust – they get punished for breaching the trust terms and/or their obligations under the trust. Once they have met these obligations – no action may be founded against the trustee. This may sound blindingly obvious, and it is, but sometimes it can be quite complicated. Say we have a trust that obliges the trustee to invest in the stock market. They perform their obligations well under the trust terms and invest according to sound strategy. For whatever reason, their investments do not turn a profit and the trust funds are therefore diminished. Despite the shoddiness of the investments, because the trustee performed their actions adequately, there can be no action against the trustee by the beneficiaries.

(d) Investment Powers: Note that as a general proposition, the trustee/s of trust property are bound to make the property profitable for the beneficiaries. They are under this duty

---

[275] *Speight v Gaunt* [1883] UKHL 1 (Lord Blackburn).
[276] *Morley v Morley* (1678) 22 ER 817 (Lord Nottingham LC).

to invest should the proper construction of the trust tell them to do so. The term 'making the trust profitable' will pretty much only be excluded in situations whereby it would be counterproductive or useless to do so. Let's say I contract you to be my broker, outside trading hours, to buy some shares for me. In doing so, I advance you a sum of money, to be held on trust to make that happen. It would be rather ridiculous for the broker to be bound to make the trust funds profitable in the interim period between transfer and when they buy the shares for me. Naturally, the opposite answer is true for the trustees of a long-term fund. Let's say this time that they oversee a pension fund. The proposition that this bunch of trustees will be excluded from the duty to invest is as absurd a notion as the previous case having that very same duty answered in the affirmative. Of course, the settlor (the dude making the trust, apparently now a unisex term) may avoid all of this uncertainty by just expressly stating what their wishes are in the trust document.

Regarding the standard of care within the powers of investment; there is now legislation guiding the way. The *Trustee Act*[277] again reiterates the trustee's power of investment. However, the statute also leaves intact the final decision-making prerogative of the settlor to enforce their true intent (of what the trust should be ultimately for).[278] The main issue dealt with through this statute is the standard of care that the trustee/s ought to reach to successfully discharge their duties. For a trustee that is not a member of a profession which ordinary acts as a trustee, the duty is *slightly* changed, being by reference to the ordinary and prudent man[279] (slightly different from the standard enumerated in *Gaunt*).[280] For a trustee within such a profession (such as lawyers, financial managers, and so on) the standard is to a higher level – by reference to an ordinary member of that profession.[281] This distinction is a fair one; giving those with a higher level of knowledge a correspondingly higher standard by which to achieve. It also increases the chance a settlor would choose a member of such an occupation to be trustee; thereby limiting the propensity by which those without the requisite knowledge may be placed in such a position (another positive). The standard also gives some leeway through the requirement that the duty of care is only by reference to the profession the trustee is a member of (and not the aggregate

---

[277] *Trustee Act 1925* (NSW) s 14.
[278] Ibid.
[279] Ibid s 14A(2)(b).
[280] *Speight v Gaunt* [1883] UKHL 1 (Lord Blackburn).
[281] *Trustee Act 1925* (NSW) s 14A(2)(a).

of all occupations ordinarily acting as trustees). Lawyers, for example, are not held to the same standard regarding knowledge of finance or financial instruments as mangers of capital firms. Likewise, financial managers are not held to have the same level of knowledge regarding the operation of the law as a solicitor.

The final issues the statute deals with (for our purposes) are the numerous factors which may be taken into account by the person wielding an investment power within the process of investment. The section is effectively a restatement of rules sourced from the equitable courts and includes duties to maximise return for each class (income and capital) of beneficiary, to not seek volatile investments, and other very vanilla duties.[282] In law school I wouldn't ever really go through each duty (except when revising for exams). The duties are so blindingly obvious. Basically, the duties can be summarised as: 'maximise returns over the long term for everyone and don't do anything stupid in the meantime.'

(e) *Other Duties:* There exist a fair few more duties which I won't go into, just note they are there. As such, the above analysis is incomplete when regarding what the trustee/s must do and the standard they are held to (when acting within their capacity as trustee). Some of these include the duty to act personally, unanimously, independantly and evermore still.

3 *Beneficiary Powers*

(a) *Information:* As already mentioned above, the beneficiaries are entitled to an account from the trustees. They may also request (and be granted access to) other information subject to the information not being confidential by any reason (such as under legal privilege). Examples of these limitations include the trust instrument (expressly or impliedly) limiting access. As mentioned, anything to do with discretion is typically off limits to the beneficiaries.

---

[282] Ibid s 14C.

(b) *Gifts:* Should the beneficiaries be adults (and otherwise capable of entering legal relations – e.g. suffering from no mental disabilities) then they may gift or sell away their interest in the trust.

(c) *Termination – 'Give me the Money Please:'* The largest power given to beneficiaries, however, is that they may (even counter to the wishes of the settlor) end the trust and force the trustee to hand over full legal title to the trust property. The precedent here dates to the leading judgment of *Saunders,*[283] in which a trust the settlor had intended to end when the beneficiary was aged 25 was terminated by the beneficiary at age 21. The consequence of the case is that beneficiary wishes (post the age of legal majority if they also be of sound mind i.e. that they be *sui juris*) will override even explicit settlor intention. The consequences of such a ruling cannot be overstated, as almost every will ever written has some kind of age restriction imposed on property transfer. Generally, a common form of testament has (should both parents pass away) property being transferred to trustees, on trust for the child until they reach some specified age over 18 (usually either 21 or 25).

This is obviously because 18-year-olds are often deemed by their parents to be unlikely to use the large windfall of property in their best long-term interests. Put another way, the settlors of such trusts deem them too immature and liable to burn through the property; hence why the higher age is imposed. This rule, however, makes the settlor's intent meaningless for these purposes. An 18-year-old in Australia (other nations may have different ages of majority), may ask (and succeed in asking), for the property to be transferred to them absolutely even though their parents (or whoever left them property) did not wish it so.

4 Rights of a Trustee

(a) *Indemnity for Expenses:* The most important of the rights given to the trustee is their ability to recoup reasonable expenses incurred from trust property; expenses which are incurred in their administration of the trust. This is a natural consequence of the office and may not be excluded by the trust instrument. I can find no clearer summary of the

---

[283] *Saunders v Vautier* (1841) 49 ER 282 (Lord Cottenham LC).

rule than from the case of *Worrall*[284] whereby Lord Eldon gave the following statement, '*It is in the nature of the office of a trustee, whether expressed in the instrument, or not, that the trust property shall reimburse him all the charges and expenses incurred in the execution of the trust. That is implied in every such deed.*'

Lord Eldon gives a similar statement in *Dawson*,[285] '*This court infuses such a clause into every will though not directed.*'

I'll give an example here to clarify the rule. Say a trustee incurs reasonable expenses on brokerage for the trust's administration of property (in this case for the management of company shares), and for which, he pays first from his own personal funds. In this case, he will be entitled to reimbursement from the trust property, to make good his own fiscal position. Regarding quantum, he is entitled to be placed back into the financial position he was in before the transaction took place.

(i) *Nature of the Right:* The extent to which this right exists is clear – it most likely acts (as stated by one of my favourite cases on the subject) as a lien or charge over the assets of the trust.[286]

However, this case references another, which perhaps admits a caveat to this rule. The caveat is that certain assets which are not permitted by the trust instrument to be utilised in continuance of the business may be excluded from the general rule (and thereby may not be utilised to indemnify the trustee).[287] For the introductory purposes of our analysis, the most important thing to note here is the proprietary nature of such a right. While we will not get into the full detail of the difference between proprietary and merely personal rights – the crux of the distinction is the ability for a proprietary right to remain and survive (in this case) the termination of trusteeship (and also bankruptcy). Effectively, this means a somewhat underhanded beneficiary may not get out of the ability for the trustee to enjoy the indemnity. No matter how hard they squirm.

---

[284] *Worrall v Harford* (1802) 8 Ves 4, 8 (Lord Eldon LC).
[285] *Dawson v Clarke* (1811) 18 Ves 247, 254.
[286] *Octavo Investments Pty Ltd v Knight* (1979) 144 CLR 360 [13].
[287] *Dowse v Gorton* [1891] AC 190, 367.

(ii) *What Expenses May Be Recovered:* The starting point, as mentioned in the above precedent (although the case in its entirety dealt on a slightly different topic) referenced above, is that the recoverable expenses must have been incurred during the administration of the trust.[288] Administration is probably taken to mean those 'proper' expenses, charges, and costs incurred in the execution of the trust.[289]

The next logical question is what exactly does 'properly' mean in these instances? The most commonly used definition is somewhat circular – being that 'properly' incurred expenses are not 'improper.' The case of *Nolan* (discussed in great depth by my law school friend group at the time we covered this in class) illustrates this rather well and goes into what expenses may/may not be recoverable.[290] The test is later expanded to be effectively that of a reasonableness inquiry regarding the trust instrument, the action the trustee was trying to execute, and their duties.[291] Even in funny illustrations such as negligent dealings by the trustee (or even the instances in which the trustee is being sued for possible breach by the beneficiaries) are likely to be recoverable. The exception for this rule is in the cases by which the trustee has acted beyond their scope of power and especially (almost definitely) in their actual fraud.

The case of *Walters* provides a good illustration of the rule. Essentially, we had a trustee that was seeking to defend their actions (as trustee) against a claim of misconduct. Once the claim was successfully defended (that is, it was shown he did not act improperly), the trustee was entitled to use trust property to reimburse himself for his own defence.[292]

My personal favourite case in showing just how far the right of indemnity goes is that of *Bennett*.[293] In this case we had a trustee operating a logging operation on some trust land. A third party was injured during the course of this logging (a tree literally fell on him) and he successfully sued the trustee. The trustee was likewise successful in gaining indemnity, against this, from trust property.

---

[288] *Octavo Investments Pty Ltd v Knight* (1979) 144 CLR 360 [35].
[289] *National Trustees Executors and Agency Company of Australasia Ltd v Barnes* (1941) 64 CLR 268, 277 (Williams J).
[290] *Nolan v Collie & Merlow Nominees Pty Ltd (In Liq)* (2003) 7 VR 287 [51] (Ormiston JA).
[291] Ibid.
[292] *Walters v Woodbridge* (1878) 7 Ch D 504.
[293] *Bennett v Wyndham* [1862] 4 De GF & J 259.

(iii) *Indemnity of Creditors:* I won't fully flesh out the law here, as it is rather complex, and the precedent has been argued to be classified as somewhat conflicting and incomplete. This being said, the basic thrust of the law here is that a creditor may have the same (in theory) right to the trustee indemnification as the trustee themselves. This is despite the *trust property* not being fully the *personal property* of the trustee (at least with regards to full beneficial ownership).

Notwithstanding the above comments, the *right of indemnity* (that a trustee enjoys) has been classified as something owned fully (including full beneficial ownership) by the trustee. Continuing with this reasoning - where do personal assets go once bankruptcy is declared? Well, they of course go to the creditor of the newly bankrupted. The proprietary asset of the indemnity of the trustee, therefore, flows like water down a hill and into the hands of their creditors. The extent to which this occurs, and who exactly is indemnified, is not, as yet, fully fleshed out by the precedent.

(iv) *Exoneration of Trustees:* Statute makes clear there are instances, in which, some breaches of a trustee may be exonerated (excused) by the court. Should a beneficiary (who is of age and sound of mind) give written consent, or instigate/request a breach of the trust by the trustees, then the court may excuse it (should the breach be reasonably conducted).[294] Likewise, the court may also make exception (or partially reduce liability), for breaches which were conducted both reasonably and honestly (or in their failure to seek directions from the court).[295] The key word in both these sections is 'may,' as in the court may or may not exclude liability. The general rule of thumb here is the more blameless the beneficiary and the higher the potential (or actual) loss caused by the breach – the less likely the court will use its discretionary powers.

---

[294] *Trustee Act 1925* (NSW) s 86.
[295] Ibid s 85.

5 Removal of Trustees

As always, I will refer you to my favourite case which lays down the general expressions of the rules. In the leading judgment of *Letterstedt*,[296] the court effectively enunciated the principle that the trustees exist 'for the benefit' of the beneficiaries. As such, departure from the proper administration of the trust may well provide sufficient reason to remove a trustee from office. The judgment continues, should the court be convinced that the 'continuance' of the trustee would endanger its proper execution, then the trustee may well be removed. Clearly any hint of dishonesty and/or impartiality will usually allow such a move – this being counter to the entire purpose of a trust. Negligence is a more delicate matter, with seemingly minor and 'one-off' type errors unlikely to attract removal, as set against repeated and/or larger infractions. Basically, the test can be summarised as - the court will likely remove the trustees if it forms the opinion that the best interest of the beneficiaries and/or the administration of the trust is better served with their removal. A perhaps harsh application of this general rule can be seen with the principle that a bankrupt trustee will almost certainly be removed from office.[297] This is regardless of how he entered financial distress – the courts taking the view that the moral hazard of permitting someone who has every material incentive to *misplace* trust property (usually despite any evidence that they will actually do so) as too high a risk upon the beneficiaries.

6 Replacing Trustees

So, we've gotten rid of a trustee and now we want a new one. The first logical question is why we even want this? Similarly, the first (second?) thing to be stated here, is the obvious point that were there only one trustee to begin with, and the beneficiaries are either too young (or otherwise incapable) of terminating the trust, then clearly a new trustee is required.

Should there have been two trustees and now there is only one; you might logically pose the next question, 'do we need another?' What I would say here is that having only one trustee is probably not all that great an idea, most notably because this increases the propensity for fraud or other financial disadvantage to be levied on the beneficiaries. Clearly, should two people's intention be needed to pilfer property (away from the proper administration of the trust); this

---

[296] *Letterstedt v Broers* (1884) 9 App Cas 371 (Lord Blackburn).
[297] *Bainbrigge v Blair* (1839) 48 ER 1032.

will be more difficult to achieve than a unilateral intent having the same ability. Moving away from direct fraud here, negligent ideas also tend to dissipate when more people are thinking about a problem. Hence, having more than a singular trustee also decreases the propensity for negligent use of trust property to occur.

Now, we move to what I would submit is the best elaboration on the factors the court will look towards in appointing a new trustee. The judgment of *Re Tempest*[298] outlines three lines of inquiry from the court's perspective regarding this question.

> *(a) Trust Instrument:* Should any intention be found from the settlor in the trust instrument, either express or implied, then the court will likely have regard to it. However, any statements or conduct (post the objective actions used in making the trust) are nigh irrelevant for this analysis.

> *(b) Furtherance of Trust Execution:* The primary inquiry needing satisfaction, in the affirmative (for the court to appoint), is whether the appointment will aid in the administration of the trust (or hinder it). Rather clearly, as mentioned above, there are numerous benefits in appointing an individual to be trust should there be otherwise only one trustee. The counter is also true, should there already be too many trustees (or enough of them), then it is unlikely the court will appoint another (as this may form a clutter of opinion in its administration). Too many cooks can spoil a broth.

> *(c) The Few Against the Many:* If one beneficiary (or a few of them) want a particular person to be trustee, and this is not supported by the settlor, or it is not in the interests of the other beneficiaries – the court will generally be reticent to appoint them to the position.

7 *Tracing Rules*

Now we begin talking about the paradigm 'remedy' for breaches of trust – that of the tracing claim. I say 'remedy' because, at least in a traditional sense, the claim is merely a reflection of the beneficiary's proprietary interest in trust property (as opposed to something like damages for loss). This distinction may provide extra assistance to the aggrieved party - as the claim

---

[298] (1866) 1 Ch App 485 (Turner LJ).

survives bankruptcy. A plaintiff, in these circumstances, will perhaps find relief in knowing they 'jump the line' ahead of every other unsecured creditor (with regards to their claim on property). On a slight side note, you never want to be an unsecured creditor in a bankruptcy claim – you are unlikely to see your money ever again my friend.

Notwithstanding the above comments, from the position of the layman plaintiff (who simply wants their money back), it's a remedy in the sense that it gives them what they want (and remedies the wrong committed). However, the fact that tracing is not a remedy in the traditional sense will rear its head in a few scenarios (which may diminish the utility to the plaintiff should a few permutations be imposed).

The following will deal with the permutations which may be observed (with regards to tracing rules). Firstly, please note there remains a difference in nomenclature between 'tracing' and 'following.' Following is what we may traditionally think of. Let's say a bundle of cash (actual notes) is the trust property. That bundle of notes is taken by the trustee and placed in their house within their own personal safe. We 'follow' this bundle of notes and claim it. Should, however, the trustee go to the bank and exchange it for digital numbers in his bank account (or buy anything with the cash) – this is where the tracing claim will arise as the money has been exchanged for a 'chose in action' against the bank (or exchanged for the good that he bought with it in the latter example). A 'chose in action' is a term used for intangible property whereby enforcement can only be ensured through the courts. That is, should someone steal physical cash from you - you can steal it back. This is contrasted to a bank account in which should the bank not allow you to withdraw - your only point of recourse is to sue them.

Tracing rights also follow the stuff which is purchased (that is not another form of money). So, in the first example, physical notes are exchanged for the chose in action against the bank. Should our hypothetical trustee breach the trust by doing something else (as slightly referenced in the first example); like buying gold bullion, or a car, or whatever - then the aggrieved beneficiary may trace (and claim) into these things as well. The ability stops, however, when the thing that was bought is used up (instead of being merely transferred into another form). So, this time, our trustee buys really expensive bars of chocolate. The plaintiff will have a proprietary claim against these bars until the point at which they are eaten. The proprietary claim in this hypothetical scenario, at the point of consumption, only extends to the chocolate wrappers (with the claim against the chocolate itself being limited down to a personal claim against the trustee). This personal claim, however, does not survive bankruptcy, and hence you will invariably join the very same line of people you really don't wish to be in.

(a) Mixed Funds: Perhaps the most common example of a breach of trust is the scenario in which the trustee withdraws funds from the trust account and puts it in their own (personal) bank account. The trust is considered, as a matter of law, to proceed despite the mixing.[299] That is, the trust continues over the mixed funds to the extent the money is an accurate reflection of the transfer from the trust account to the personal. The rule essentially has the trust continuing (not ending) despite the breach. The reasoning here is pretty obvious, otherwise how many trusts would be breached if the trustees knew that such breaches would end their obligations (and necessarily limit any proprietary claim the beneficiaries may have on the property)?

You, let's say you're the aggrieved beneficiary, will essentially retain the ability for a proprietary claim, as long as the property exists as the actual property (or the traceable substitute). Should the trustee burn through some of the mixed cash on junk – then they will be presumed to have wasted their own money first. This is a logical extension of the legal assumption in the continued existence of the trust.

One notable exception to the above scheme is in the so-called intermediate balance rule.[300] The rule holds that should trust funds be moved to another account, and that fund is depleted below the sum which was pilfered – the proprietary claim only extends to the amount where the account balance was at its lowest point (hence the name – the lowest intermediate balance).

I'll give an example here for additional clarification. Let's say the trust fund consisted of $1000, the trustee then moved this money into his own account that already had another thousand. The trustee has $2000 now - $1000 of which was trust money. At this point, should the trustee burn through any sum of money less than $1000, they will be assumed to have spent their own money first (and you retain the ability to have a

---

[299] *Re Hallett's Estate* (1880) 13 Ch D 696 (Lord Jessel MR).
[300] *James Roscoe (Bolton) Ltd v Winder* [1915] 1 Ch 62 (Sargant J); See also, for a recent Australian application of the rule, *Re French Caledonia Travel Service Pty Ltd (In Liq)* (2003) 59 NSWLR 361 (Campbell J).

proprietary claim on the remaining thousand as the representation of trust property). Should they waste more than $1000 however, you will only get access to a proprietary remedy towards the money that isn't spent. For example, the trustee spends $1500 on some junk that you can't claim into (otherwise we'd just claim the thing that was bought). In this case, you only get a proprietary remedy on $500 and a personal remedy (sue and pray he's not insolvent) for the remaining amount. This holds true even if he moves more money back into the account post 'the spend' occurring (hence the term intermediate balance).

There is an exception. Should there be evidence of an intention that any subsequent windfall of resources into the account was generated for repayment of the trust – then the rule will not apply.

It is easy to think that the rule is unfairly harsh against a blameless and wronged beneficiary. The critique is rebutted, however, through referencing the non-remedial nature of the tracing claim. Because the claim is merely a reflection of the proprietary interest in the property from the position of the beneficiary; it would be incorrect to allow for a claim against property which is by no means related to that which was pilfered or otherwise handled improperly.

(b) *Profit from Breach:* The above scenario holds whenever a trustee either mixes trust funds with their own, buys some worthless junk, or purchases something worth a fair amount (but uses it up). It is also possible if the trustee buys something with trust property which is useful (in the sense that it generates a financial return).

Should this happen, because the property (that has increased in value) is the traceable substitute of trust property, and because the tracing claim is merely a reflection of the proprietary interests of the beneficiary (instead of being a remedy to compensate for loss) - they will likewise be entitled to claim the property (that has had its value increased).[301] So, let's say the trustee stole $1000 from the trust account and used it to buy some gold. The price of gold then doubled, making it worth $2000. The beneficiary

---

[301] *Foskett v McKeown* [2001] 1 AC 102 (Lord Millet).

can claim the whole piece of gold (or company shares, or whatever investment was bought). This is instead of merely having a $1000 claim against such property.

(c) *Tracing Backwards:* Let's now suppose our trustee takes out a loan to buy a car. Sensing that he cannot repay the loan, he pilfers trust funds and repays it. The funds are dissipated (in repayment of the loan) and hence there is no recourse in following the money. The only possibility is a claim against the property that the loan was taken out to buy (which was repaid through the unauthorised use of trust funds). This is known as backwards tracing.

Backwards tracing has only been recently shown to be available for aggrieved beneficiaries within the United Kingdom (within the leading case of *Durant*).[302] This is only possible, however, should a sufficient nexus exist between the gaining of an asset and breaching of the trust fund. This being said, the precedent has not yet been applied, nor has it been accepted within the Australian jurisdiction (as yet). My own view on this score is that the proposition should be answered in the affirmative, allowing the doctrine. The reasoning here is that the 'remedy' is not a blank cheque; there still needs to be the establishment of a substantial nexus between the debt being paid and the trust in some way. This, I find (although merely a personal opinion), provides adequate protection and maintains the claim's status as a reflection of proprietary rights as opposed to a remedy.

(d) *Clayton's Rule:* I loathe *Clayton's* rule. I remember, as a law student, absolutely not understanding the rule until an example was provided in class. To save you some pain, I'll start with an example. Let's say we have a trustee to multiple beneficiaries - Augustus, Belisarius, Caesar, and Dickus. They each have $50 on trust. The trustee takes the $50 from Augustus and deposits it into his personal bank account – which has $50 of his own already in it. He does the same then with the $50 from Belisarius, then from Caesar, and finally from Dickus. His account now has $250 in it. He then spends $151 on some junk that he uses up (and hence we can't trace into).

The traditional rule, under *Clayton's Case*[303] has it assumed that the trustee 'uses up' his money first, and then first uses up the first moneys from the beneficiaries in the

---

[302] *The Federal Republic of Brazil v Durant International Corporation (Jersey)* [2015] UKPC 35 [40] (Lord Toulson).
[303] *Devaynes v Noble* (1816) 35 ER 767 (Grant MR).

order that they entered his account. So, in this case, the first $50 would be his own, the next $50 would be Augustus' entire account, and then the entire of Belisarius' balance, and then $1 from Caesar. So, this case would have Augustus without any remaining traceable property (all $50 gone), the same with Belisarius (all $50 gone), Caesar would be able to trace $49, and lucky Dickus could trace his entire $50.

How does this make sense?

Thankfully newer decisions (particularly in Australia – but in England as well, albeit with more careful wording by English jurists) have viewed the traditional doctrine with significant scepticism. Newer judgments will, therefore, typically apply a pro rata adjustment to the calculations and spread the loss across all the impacted beneficiaries.

E *Equitable Remedies*

Okay, so we now begin our discussion here with two general precepts. Namely that while common law damages are available as of right; equitable remedies are discretionary. Also, the method for calculation, for the remedies, are also somewhat unsettled.

1 *Bars to Remedy*

   (a) *Unclean Hands:* The most famous discretionary barrier to remedy is that a plaintiff with 'unclean hands' may well be unable (effectively meaning undeserving by view of the court) to receive it. The wrong committed by the plaintiff needs to have some type of nexus between it and the right the plaintiff is trying to enforce. This is opposed to some more general (and unrelated) immorality. So, for example, a plaintiff who was attempting to enforce some estoppel against his business partner will not be barred because he cheated on his wife. He will, however, likely be barred against remedy if he has committed a related fraud of some type on the same business partner. The maxim has been stated, rather eloquently in *Meyers,*[304] to be such that a plaintiff may be barred

---

[304] *Meyers v Casey* (1913) 17 CLR 90, 124 (Isaacs J).

in circumstances in which the granting of a remedy will be aiding or 'protecting' the wrong they have committed. My favourite illustration of the rule in is the old case of *Overton*,[305] in which, the child beneficiaries were barred from a remedy against their trustee (for breach of trust) because they had misrepresented their age to the trustee and induced him into it.

(b) *Laches - Expedit Reipublicae Ut Sit Finis Litium:* Laches are taken by some bad legal textbooks (and a ton of university student notes) to simply mean that delay of an unreasonable length blocks the plaintiff from receiving remedy. This is only partway true. The starting point of the discussion must begin with *Smith*,[306] in which the equitable remedy was denied. This was due to the breach occurring many decades before the case was litigated. The judgment of this case has been used in supporting the idea that time alone will be sufficient in creating laches. What I will say here is that the case is unique (and does not reflect the current state of the law) in two ways:

(i) *Age:* The case is of the late 18th century. When the judgment was laid down here, the 13 colonies were still firmly in the hands of the British and Queen Victoria hadn't yet been born (and wouldn't be for around half a century).

(ii) *Legislative Issues:* The case wasn't purely an issue for the Court of Chancery. It had, within it, issues of time limitations laid down in statute (statutes of limitations). Therefore, it may have been decided on its own facts.

The current state of the law is more accurately described in the judgement of *Lindsay*;[307] whereby two limbs of the doctrine were enunciated.

(i) *Delay:* There must be some delay. The timeframe of which will be a useful factor, yet not a conclusive one.
(ii) *Practical Unjustness:* The delay must cause some type of unfairness between the parties. For example, in the interim period since the breach, the defendant has carried on their affairs (and now the loss is greater than if the plaintiff had utilised

---

[305] *Overton v Banister* (1844) 3 Hare 503.
[306] *Smith v Clay* (1767) 29 ER 743 (Lord Camden LC).
[307] *Lindsay Petroleum Co v Hurd* [1874] LR 5 PC 221 (Lord Selbourne LC).

their rights when the wrong was committed). Another, more obvious example, is that since the breach, evidence of the wrong (or defences to it) were lost.

(c) *Hardship:* Should the remedy sought be unreasonably harsh on the defendant (for example due to some change in the circumstances since the wrong was committed) then the courts generally will seek to impose one as causing less detriment to such a defendant. The principle is best stated by Chief Justice Griffith in the case of *Dowsett*,[308]

'The Court is not bound to enforce a bargain which would work great hardship upon either party.'

Perhaps the most famous case illustrating the rule (and my personal favourite that was discussed in class) here is *Patel*,[309] in which the remedy of specific performance (the remedy would have removed her from her house) was rejected. This was due to the defendant being diagnosed with cancer, becoming significantly disabled due to this, and receiving significant support from neighbours which aided her throughout the illness. Such a remedy was deemed far too harsh for a court of equity to impose.

I'm going to go on a slight tangent here to speak about the current pension and housing system in Australia. During my tenure as a law student, I was involved in a mentor type program with a big law firm. During such time, the mentor I was paired up with (and I) got into a discussion regarding housing in Australia (this mentor at the time was buying a property). Somehow, we got onto the topic of whether the 'primary place of residence' (the family home) should be included into the asset calculation test for receiving the pension – currently it is not. I was against such a move, and my mentor was for it. The argument utilised to push for such a measure was that it is economically inefficient (for both government budgets and in placing upward pressure on housing prices) to have grandmothers living alone in expensive homes (when they could sell them and move into someplace smaller). I'm going to perhaps surprise most of you and say that this is totally and completely true (it is very inefficient). That being said, I am still dead against such a measure. The reasoning is pretty simple, my grandmother is now very frail, and her short-term memory is also failing. Any time she wakes up in some new place, she has invariably forgotten how she got there, and then freaks out – becoming very

---

[308] *Dowsett v Reid* (1912) 15 CLR 695, 705-6 (Griffith CJ).
[309] *Patel v Ali* [1984] 1 All ER 978.

distressed and afraid. Nothing settles her down like being in her own home, the only place in the world she feels safe these days. Needless to say, she, being a stalwart of her community, also receives significant aid and companionship from her neighbourhood; of which she has contributed to her entire adult life. The community also has a large migrant population of the same age, which speaks the same language, which she can communicate with. Forced removal from her home would be efficient, but at what cost? I know for certain that it would hugely diminish her standard of life, decrease the care she receives, and make her both afraid and lonely simultaneously. It would almost certainly shorten her life. This is something I cannot countenance nor support. And this isn't coming from some leftie; you'll only hear support of tree trade from me (as described in my first book) as an example of my 'libertarian street cred.' There are just some lines I will not cross. Making senior citizens lives miserable and diminishing their happiness (in the twilight of their years) is one of them.

As I write subsequent edits to this book – my grandmother has since passed on. Nearer to the end than when I first wrote this book, she became even more frail and even more confused. Eventually, we had to move her into a nursing home to receive proper and full-time care. She missed her home though. She missed it dearly.

I miss her too.

(d) *Third Parties:* Courts of equity will also consider the impact of their orders on third parties. Should the sought remedy be too harsh on innocent bystanders, the order is generally moulded to not be so intrusive on the rights or interests of others. An example here is given in the recent case of *John Alexander's*,[310] in which the court referred to its hesitancy (in this case in the granting of a constructive trust) in impacting the rights of those unrelated to the matter at hand. The doctrine not only impacts which remedies the court will impose – but also how it will impose them. For example, in *Dodds* Justice Deane stated the date from which a constructive trust would be imposed should be altered due to third party interests otherwise being impacted.

'Lest the legitimate claims of third parties be adversely affected, the constructive trust should be imposed only from the date of publication of reasons for judgment of this Court.'[311]

---

[310] *John Alexander's Clubs Pty Ltd v White City Tennis Club Ltd* (2010) 241 CLR 1 [129].
[311] *Muschinski v Dodds* (1985) 160 CLR 583 (Deane J).

(e) Minimum Equity: This isn't a bar to remedy so much as it is a reflection of the locus by which the court follows in granting equitable relief. The starting point for this assessment is presented within the leading judgment of *Crabb*,[312] whereby the court enunciated the preferable remedy as that which is the minimum required to do 'justice' to the plaintiff. Justice in this instance meaning the plaintiff receiving the equitable right which they are judged to hold.[313]

What the minimum equity entails is of intense judicial discussion (and a recent slew of matters in equitable estoppel have shown peculiarities within that particular species of case). The leading case here (showing the difficulty of the minimum equity principle in the area of equitable estoppel), within Australia, is *Giumelli*,[314] in which the High Court accepts and expands on an earlier case.[315] It reinforces the notion that the equity required to do justice, in these instances, is prima facie (subject to rebuttal from surrounding circumstances – such as effect on third parties) that of enforcing the promise made between the parties.[316] This is a reflection of these matters being caused primarily by the unconscionability for the defendant to not 'stick to their word' and 'go through' with the promise which they have made. The court will not, however, make a judgment which goes beyond that which would have been considered conscionable conduct by the defendant.[317]

2 *Different Types of Remedy*

There are a few preliminaries which need to be dealt with before we delve into some substantial law within this section. Firstly, the equitable remedies are not conclusively listed below, this section merely deals with the most common (and truth be told, the ones which I find most interesting to write about as well) examples. Also note that rescission (also available here) has already been dealt with (in an earlier section of the book). The final thing to be stated, is that

---

[312] *Crabb v Arunn District Council* [1975] EWCA Civ 7 (Scarman LJ).
[313] Ibid.
[314] *Giumelli v Giumelli* (1999) 196 CLR 101.
[315] *The Commonwealth v Verwayen* (1990) 170 CLR 394.
[316] *Giumelli v Giumelli* (1999) 196 CLR 101 [40]-[50].
[317] Ibid.

as assessed above, there is a large distinction between personal remedies and those of a proprietary nature – the latter surviving bankruptcy.

> *(a) Rectification:* Where a document does not truly reflect the final agreement of the parties (there need be clear evidence of this and what the true intentions were) the plaintiff may succeed (subject to the bars above) in having the court change the document to reflect such intentions.
>
> The old case of *Fowler* perhaps has the most well summarised form of the rule,
>
> *'Only after the court has been satisfied by evidence which leaves no 'fair and reasonable doubt' that the deed impeached does not embody the final intention of the parties. This evidence must make it clear that the alleged intention to which the plaintiff asks that the deed be made to conform, continued concurrently in the minds of all the parties down to the time of its execution; and the plaintiff must succeed in showing also the precise form in which the instrument will express this intention.'*[318]
>
> *(b) Specific Performance:* There is an agreement between two parties. Post the agreement being made, one of them (through conduct or words) communicates to the other that they are reluctant in executing their side of a bargain. Where damages are inadequate,[319] specific performance will be available as a remedy to enforce the agreement. The central issue here, for the prima facie ability of specific performance to be available, is that of the inadequacy of other remedies. There are many reasons why damages may be deemed inadequate, such as a presumption in the affirmative (for specific performance availability) for contracts of land (based on the notion that no two pieces of land are identical). Chattels on the other hand will generally not (but sometimes will) attract the remedy.[320] This is unless they are exceptionally rare, or some shortage exists, or there is little chance (but-for specific performance being granted) that the plaintiff will receive their goods on time. Just note the biggest bar to the award of specific performance (a unique barrier, in addition to the above bars) is that a high necessity of court supervision (in ensuring performance) will almost certainly deny the plaintiff

---

[318] *Fowler v Fowler* (1859) 4 De G & J 250, 264-5. As a side note – I thank Wikipedia for providing me the exact quote. I remembered it, vaguely, when writing the book, but for the life of me could not find any resource having the exact quote. I then stumbled upon Wikipedia, where the quote, in its entirety, was mercifully there.
[319] *Falcke v Gray* (1859) 62 ER 250.
[320] Ibid.

from the remedy.[321] This is due to the courts being fundamentally unequipped to supervise proper performance of contracts, as opposed to (as a countervailing example) their ability to award other remedies such as damages.

A good example of this rule is in the case of *Mutual Tontine*[322] whereby the court refused to specifically enforce a contract that required a man to consistently be performing a specific job. Because this would have required the court to be constantly checking whether this job was being performed – the court refused this particular remedy.

(c) *Injunctions:* Injunctions restrict conduct. That is, they stop the defendant from beginning (or carrying on with) something that imposes upon the rights of the plaintiff. Likewise to the above analysis, damages need be an inadequate remedy for the granting of an injunction.[323] Also note injunctions come in a few flavours.

> (i) *Ordinary Restraining Injunctions:* This is the most common form of injunction granted. Say you are conducting a wrong which infringes on the rights or interests of the plaintiff. This wrong will also probably continue but-for the court intervening (by the granting of an injunction). Damages are also insufficient. The court, in this scenario, will likely grant the plaintiff the injunction they seek to ensure that you cannot keep doing what you are doing.
>
> By way of illustration - let's say I'm digging up my backyard to fix my sewer pipes, and in doing so I happen to start preparing to smash up the common pipe which goes down the backyards of everyone in the street. My neighbour notices me preparing to damage the sewer systems of the entire neighbourhood and asks for an injunction. Let's say the court grants it (the court probably would in this instance). The injunction would be an order to stop me from continuing in my dastardly plan to destroy the pipe. Please also note that I don't have to *intentionally* be doing something harmful/idiotic. Even if my plan was unintentional (e.g. I thought I was correctly fixing my plumbing issue) – the court can still impose the injunction.

---

[321] *JC Williamson Ltd v Lukey and Mulholland* (1931) 45 CLR 282 (Dixon J).
[322] *Ryan v Mutual Tontine Westminster Chambers Association* (1893) 1 Ch 116.
[323] *Hogg v Kirby* [1803] EngR 513 (Lord Eldon LC).

(ii) *Quia Timet Injunctions:* Here the wrong has not yet occurred, but the plaintiff is fearful of such an imposition on their rights or interests, and hence seeks to pre-emptively remove the threat. The leading judgment here is *Fletcher* in which the rules for such injunctions were laid out.[324] There needs to be sufficient evidence of imminent danger, proof the damage will be substantial and/or irreparable, and that the plaintiff would be unable to defend themselves against the wrong (should the plaintiff be denied such a remedy).

My favourite illustration of the rule is in *Frost*[325] whereby a big rock was placed by mother nature precariously on a cliff and above a home. The owners of the home below were understandably very scared about this big rock that could fall upon them at essentially any time. Please also note that the case decided a lot of other stuff as well (such as the law of nuisance) and its complete judgment is not overly useful to our purposes here. That being said, the court stated that this is an example (of a fact pattern) where *quia timet* relief may apply *in principle* – giving the homeowners pre-emptive rights (because the boulder has not yet fallen) to remove the stone.[326]

(iii) *Interim/Interlocutory Injunctions:* These injunctions are those ordered at the beginning of a court process (to be in force while it commences). So the plaintiff complains about some wrong committed by the defendant and asks the court to impose restrictions on the conduct of the defendant while proceedings are commenced (to restrict damage to the plaintiff in the interim period). My own favourite case of *NWL*[327] has the leading judgment delve into the balancing act the court must dance in reaching its conclusion as whether to grant the remedy or not. Effectively, the court must discern whether the damage to the plaintiff will be higher in not granting the injunction (with the addition of the possibility of damages for the intermediate period included within this calculus) when compared to the damage to the defendant (in granting the remedy). The court will likely make such an order if the former is decided as higher. If the contrary is true, in this 'balance of convenience,' the court will be unlikely to grant the

---

[324] *Fletcher v Bealey* (1885) 28 Ch D 688 (Pearson J).
[325] *Frost v Northern Beaches Council* [2022] NSWSC 1214.
[326] Ibid [25].
[327] *NWL Ltd v Woods* [1979] 3 All ER 614 (Lord Diplock).

relief sought. Similarly, the court must look towards the odds that the party seeking the injunction is likely to succeed at trial. The more likely they are to succeed – the more likely that they will be granted injunctive relief in the interim period.[328]

- (iv) *Mandatory Injunctions:* While most injunctions restrain conduct, some are to force it. The difference between this and specific performance is that the former forces action outside of an agreement and the latter within them. The paradigm example where this relief may be available is where the defendant's conduct caused something to bugger up (i.e. they have probably damaged something) and the plaintiff wants to force the defendant to fix it (as opposed to getting damage for the loss caused). Again, damages need to be insufficient. Also, likewise to our analysis for specific performance, should there be a high necessity for court supervision (to ensure the defendant fixes his screw up), the remedy will not likely be granted.

(d) *Equitable Damages:* The general rule was once that a court of equity was unable to grant damages, these being a common law remedy. The *Chancery Amendment Act,*[329] most commonly referred to as the *Lord Cairns' Act,* allowed the courts of equity to grant damages (in addition to, or in lieu of, other equitable forms of relief – most notably specific performance or injunctions). The *Supreme Court Act*[330] of my jurisdiction (New South Wales) does the same thing and specifically mentions injunction and specific performance. Should specific performance or an injunction not be allowable for whatever reason, but the court nonetheless remains convinced that the plaintiff is deserving of some remedy, damages here will be available. Likewise, should the remedy granted (such as an injunction) not totally relieve the plaintiff of the defendant's wrongdoing, damages (in addition) may be granted.

(e) *Constructive Trust:* Should trust property be taken from the trust accounts (and a tracing/following claim is successful) the plaintiff may be entitled to hold the property

---

[328] Ibid.
[329] *1858* (UK) 21 & 22 Vict. C 27.
[330] *1970* (NSW) s 68.

(or its traceable substitute) on trust (with the same terms as the initial one). 'Constructive' is simply a term meaning that it is the court (instead of the parties) which creates the trust. This is a common remedy for these types of equitable wrongs. The remedy may also be used as a species of cause of action in certain circumstances, of which this book (at the risk of losing its brevity), will not describe. Google 'common intention' and '*Baumgartner*' trusts for a more complete analysis. Also note that there is a discussion within academic opinion in whether the trust is a 'remedy' or an 'institution.' The former opinion is that the trust is created on court declaration. Whereas the latter is more akin to the trust always being in existence from the moment the wrong was committed. The court, in this view, merely 'declares' its existence in a similar fashion as it 'declares' jurisdictional error in administrative law. Most Australian cases provide support for the former, and almost all English decisions the latter. The final thing I will mention, on this distinction, is that should the trust be considered institutional - this will significantly impede (nigh remove) the ability for the court to not implement the discretionary order. If the constructive trust has *always* existed, on what grounds does the court have to deny its implementation?

(f) *Account of Profits:* For breaches of trust or fiduciary duties whereby the trustee or fiduciary makes an unauthorised profit in the position of their office; the plaintiff may be entitled (subject to the court's discretionary powers) to have the profit 'disgorged' and given to the plaintiff as an account of profits. The leading case of *Regal*,[331] rather forcefully, reinforces the notion that it is not through dishonesty or lack of bona fides (which makes the remedy available to the plaintiff), but instead, it is the unauthorised nature of the profits which makes it accountable.

As eloquently stated by Lord Russel of Killowen,
'My Lords - with all respect I think there is a misapprehension here. The rule of equity which insists on those who by use of a fiduciary position make a profit, being liable to account for that profit, in no way depends upon fraud, or absence of bona fides; or upon such questions or considerations as whether the profit would or should otherwise have gone to the Plaintiff, or whether the profiteer was under a duty to obtain the source of the profit for the Plaintiff, or whether he took a risk or acted as he did for the benefit of the Plaintiff, or whether the Plaintiff has in fact been damaged or benefited by his action. The liability arises from the mere fact of

---

[331] *Regal (Hastings) Ltd v Gulliver* [1967] 2 AC 134.

a profit, having, in the stated circumstances, been made. The profiteer, however honest and well intentioned, cannot escape the risk of being called upon, to account.'[332]

This may seem unduly harsh against a trustee or fiduciary who makes a profit, both for themselves *and* the beneficiary or principal (or makes a profit in the total absence of fraud). There is a high likelihood however, in these cases, that the court will make what is known as an 'allowance' (whereby the defendant will be compensated for their exercise of care, skill, and work in the generation of the profit). This was seen in *Boardman*[333] where the fiduciary utilised *excellent* business nous to make large profits for his beneficiaries. There was also significant evidence he performed his duties in good faith. He was awarded substantial allowances for his efforts. What is interesting, however, is that the leading Australian case on the matter (one which will be discussed in every law class on this subject – as it was discussed thoroughly in mine), *Warman*,[334] had the court make such an allowance even in the circumstances of significant dishonesty on the part of the fiduciary. Perhaps this is akin to a more general principle that it would (maybe) be unconscionable for a plaintiff to receive all of the profit (some of which not being directly related to the breach). Naturally, allowances made when the trustee or fiduciary was acting without fraud (or in the best interests of their charge), are generated as more princely than if some degree of dishonesty was involved. This being said, I've never really liked the outcome of *Warman*. In my view, allowances should only be possible if there is absolute good faith in the actions of the fiduciary and/or trustee. Otherwise, we have a situation whereby there is an *active incentive* for fiduciaries to breach their duties – knowing that even in cases of dishonesty they can be compensated for their efforts.

A dishonest fiduciary gains access to funds and/or other resources that they would not otherwise have access to, they breach their duties knowingly, and they are compensated for the privilege – that has never, in my mind, seemed the right approach for the courts of equity to take.

It just seems off to me.

---

[332] Ibid (Lord Russel of Killowen).
[333] *Boardman v Phipps* [1966] UKHL 2.
[334] *Warman International Ltd v Dwyer* (1995) 182 CLR 544.

Please also make a note, now, that should an account of profits or equitable compensation (below) be available to the plaintiff – an opportunity of election between the two is granted to the aggrieved party. Any lawyer worth their salt will then, of course, advise they select the option by which the plaintiff will get the higher sum.

(g) *Equitable Compensation:* This is probably the most commonly used remedy in the equitable jurisdiction (within the cases involving breach of trust or fiduciary duties).

The paradigm case here is as follows. There is a relationship between the parties (of one of the categories listed above) and the duties of which are breached. This breach causes a financial loss for the plaintiff. The plaintiff then sues to make good this loss. There is a distinction here between equitable compensation and common law remedies (namely damages). Equitable compensation does not attract the common law additions (to calculus) that the plaintiff may have contributed to the loss or should have mitigated it. Such a move would effectively be placing, upon individuals who should have the ability to place a high degree of trust in another, the requirement of still checking that their own interests are maintained. This would be counter to the entire purpose of fiduciary law (that certain classes of relationship should have unilateral duties imposed on them).

There is a further distinction between the two scenarios in which equitable compensation may be called for. This is a difference in the manner, by which, the level of compensation is calculated. The two differing methods are shown in the divergence between the types of breaches that may be encountered. Just note the overall objective of both methods is still to place the aggrieved party in the place they would have been in (had the breach not occurred).

(i) *Misapplication of Trust Property:* The first flavour of breach is the most obvious; a trustee uses trust property in a manner that was not authorised by the trust instrument (and this in some way causes a loss). These types of breach have the sum of compensation determined more strictly - with questions of causation being limited to what is effectively the but-for analysis. That is, but-for the breach, would the loss have occurred?

The cases here always have facts which leave you speechless. Mostly, the cases here have money or other property being handed over to the trustees (either for safekeeping or for the trustee to purchase something with it). The property is then stolen (or is otherwise somehow treated in a manner inconsistently, generally very inconsistently, with the trust terms).

My favourite case in this category is *Libertarian*.[335] The judgment here sums up the rule rather succinctly, whereby, should a breach of this manner occur - the defendant will be ordered to 'make good' the trust (not by compensation for loss). 'Making good' requires a restitution, of the objective value (with hindsight), of what the trust would have been worth (had the breach not occurred).[336] It is essentially a manifestation of the duty to account on the part of the trustee (of which we spoke about earlier).

The distinction can be clarified in the following example. So, let's say you give me $1000 on trust (for me to invest in some particular company). I then take the money and spend it on something useless (which takes the value down to zero). Had I invested the money in the company, as obliged, the shares would now have a value of $5000. If this doctrine was purely about loss, the amount I would be liable for is clear, you have lost $1000. However, because this doctrine obliges me to 'make good the trust' (with hindsight of what it would have been worth) - I am forced to pay the full $5000. This is because the higher amount is a more accurate reflection of the trust's value had the breach not occurred. As we can see; the impact of external variations (in value) are less important here than if a question of remoteness was imposed. The distinction will be made clearer still as we move to the next category of equitable compensation.

(ii) *Other Fiduciary Breaches:* So, while the above category deals with the misapplication of property, we are concerned here (instead) with a broader range of breaches. Namely, any other type of breach which causes the plaintiff some form of loss.

---

[335] *Libertarian Investments Ltd v Hall* [2013] HKCFA 93.
[336] Ibid (Lord Millet).

The paradigm case, here, is some type of breach of the conflicts rule (the duty that a fiduciary does not have conflicting interests in their dealings as fiduciary). This breach, naturally, then causes the plaintiff some type of loss.

An example of a set of facts, which may be illustrative here, is during dealings with a financial broker. They make representations regarding the high utility in purchasing some form of investment. They do not disclose, however, that they have a vested interest (in some way) in seeing the plaintiff pay the highest (rather than the lowest) price. The difference between what they actually paid, and the lowest possible price, can be considered a loss.

The starting point is again the overall objective to put the plaintiff where they would have been; but-for the breach. That being said, this is a harder task to accomplish than in the above category. It is exceedingly obvious what caused the loss in a property pilfering case – the loss being caused by the stealing or otherwise misapplying the property. The amount is also far clearer, being by reference to factors such as the initial value of the trust, and what it would have been (by reference to objective markers such as the market price of shares) had the breach not happened. In this calculus, however, we are often stuck in the land of the subjective. For example, in the above scenario, what really is the lowest price our broker could have possibly gotten our plaintiff (if they had been properly doing their job)?

Such a calculation is often a difficult one to make.

As contrasted with the above test (in addition to the but-for analysis) we also have 'common sense' being included here as well. As in, once the but-for test is satisfied, we must also ask by reference to common sense whether (or not) the loss was caused by the breach. Therefore, questions of external influence upon value are far more relevant in this type of scenario than above.

So, for example, we have a 'secret commission' type of case. The plaintiff receives some advice from a fiduciary (and unbeknownst to them, the person giving them the advice was receiving payment every time an advisee bought one of the spruiked products). The plaintiff then buys the product as advised (let's say it was an investment of some type). Post this purchase, there is a massive global downturn in the value of investments (such as in the Global Financial Crisis of 2008/9). There is also some evidence, that but-for the advice, the plaintiff probably wouldn't have invested in this particular product (or any product at all). If the previous test for calculating quantum was utilised, as in the misapplication of trust property cases, then the broker would likely have to pay the full amount - including whatever value was lost due to the global recession. As a matter common sense, however, the external downturn is taken into account for the purposes of equitable compensation (the quantum of which). This means that the defendant, here, is unlikely to be forced into paying for any amount of loss caused by the global downturn (their payment being limited to the breach itself – and not any amount caused by the external factors).

VIII TORT LAW

As an introduction, we'll begin this section by noting the distinction here between tort and criminal law. Criminal law matters are between the offender and the state, the primary victim of which being the Queen's (Or King's) peace. This breach to the Queen's peace is caused via their relevant wrongdoing to the individual victim (their physical acts or omissions). Punishment and enforcement, therefore, is doled out by the state; with the victim having very little say in whether (or not) the matter is prosecuted (or what the sentence should be). Tort law, to the contrary, is a matter strictly between the two parties as a *civil issue* – the plaintiff having the sole ability to choose whether to pursue the matter against whoever has wronged them (or not). This distinction is despite the fact that the actions of the defendant in tort may also overlap (nearly exactly) with their criminal counterparts. Assault, for example, being the paradigm tort case (with the oldest history) and likewise having endless permutations in criminal law as well. Naturally, the punishments available to a civil plaintiff are more limited in scope than those that the state might employ, with (apart from an injunction stopping particular behaviour), individuals in civil matters not having any ability of imprisonment or otherwise restraining the further actions of the defendant. This chapter is a non-exhaustive list of the available torts.

There is also some nomenclature we must also discuss before delving into the substantive law. Firstly, there is a distinction between torts that are known as *intentional* (such as assault and false imprisonment) and those born of negligence. The second and perhaps more important distinction is in the divergence in what the tort is against. Assault (including battery) and false imprisonment are torts against the person – meaning that you have the ability to sue despite there being no damages (with Western nations typically placing a high value on mere bodily integrity and freedom from external interference). Other torts, protecting the integrity of things other than the person itself, may well require proof of damage as a prerequisite for the court process to begin.

A final note should be made regarding the standard of proof – being the balance of probabilities (with the burden falling on the plaintiff).

A *Intentional Assault*

Similar to the analysis in criminal law, we have the ability for an assault to constitute both physical contact (named battery), and mere threats.

(a) Non-Physical: The tort is effectively made out should the defendant make a threat in which causes the plaintiff to reasonably (meaning an objective test) fear (most cases use the term 'apprehend') imminent and unlawful bodily interference. The use of the objective test has the natural consequence that the plaintiff need have been aware of the threat being made. That is, if they didn't receive the threat (say they never got the message), or they could not have received the threat (for example they were unconscious when it was made), or knew the threat was nought but air (let's say they knew the knife presented was plastic) - then there is no assault. Clearly it must also be unconsented. I will use two cases to illustrate the point here.

   (i) Words or Conduct of an Assault: The words or conduct need make the plaintiff reasonably apprehend immediate violence – hence threats regarding future violence generally do not attract a remedy.

   As an illustration, the conduct of police in the case of *Ibbett*[337] was sufficient to meet this threshold, with the defendant (unlawfully) entering a house while in pursuit an individual (that may have committed a crime). The officer then produced a gun towards the direction of an elderly third party (the owner of the home). This is a most obvious illustration of the rule – having a gun pointed at you being perhaps the highest level of threat available (of all possible flavours). The assault was therefore made out.

   (ii) Getting out of an Assault: I think the favourite assault case of any law student is that of *Tuberville,*[338] whereby there were some insulting comments made from plaintiff to defendant. The insulted party (defendant) then placed his hand on his sword and said something to the effect of, 'if it were not for the time, I would not take such language from you.' Will putting your hand on your sword in a threatening manner (especially in the modern age where nobody wears

---

[337] *State of New South Wales v Ibbett* (2005) 65 NSWLR 168.
[338] *Tuberville v Savage* [1669] EWHC KB J25.

them) normally constitute an assault? Well, the answer is clearly in the affirmative. The funny thing here is that the defendant was not found liable. The reasoning is that should you properly construct his statement – he was saying he *would not* harm the plaintiff and thereby there could not have been an assault. I would not recommend trying this, as more recent cases have gone the other way – with even conditional threats being constructed as being able to cause, within another, a fear of imminent harm.

(b) *Battery:* This is a far easier topic. The defendant need only impose unlawful contact on another. Unlawful meaning not consented to (although with the caveat that there is some harm that can never have consent – similar to our assessment for criminal assault). The contact need also be outside of what is considered ordinary in the circumstances. So, walking into a music festival (in the crowd) will ordinarily attract some rubbing of shoulders – this will not be an assault. The law recognises the need to identify 'ordinary' types of behaviour (in different circumstances) that would make this type of conduct lawful within one context versus unlawful in another. Similarly, should contact take place within the context of reasonable self-defence – this conduct is also not at all unlawful.

The other thing I will say within this area is that an assault must be an act. It cannot be an omission. The most famous case here (both in tort and criminal law – for its judgment and its ridiculous facts) is probably *Fagan*.[339] Essentially, we had a guy drive accidentally onto a policeman's leg, and then, for whatever reason, didn't drive off. The court constructed the positive act as his choice to not remove himself from the foot of the officer.

The lesson to be learned here is that if the court wants to get you – they will find a way to get you.

---

[339] *Fagan v Metropolitan Police Commissioner* [1968] 3 All ER 442 (James J).

B *Conversion and Trespass*

The above torts deal with the rights of the person. The following (which will be dealt with rather briefly) are civil wrongs in relation to the actions of the defendant (which contravene the rights of a plaintiff) with regard to property. Please also note that there are some more complex rules regarding how these torts interrelate to bailment of goods. Bailment is effectively the handing over of goods (from someone with at least actual possession) to be held by another.

The best example I can think of (for bailment) is the temporary seizure of, along with the right to retrieve, my personal 'Swiss Army' knife when I travel inside the court complex.

To be given legal access to the building, I must hand over my knife to the security guards for safekeeping. When I'm done with whatever I was doing, for example my Roman law class (one of my final law school subjects - a brilliant class by the way), I will retrieve my knife and leave the building. While the knife is in the custody of the guards – this is considered as a bailment of the knife.

Note that a bailment may either be for or without consideration (that is, a bailment may be free or in return for something) and that those who gain the goods also generally gain (subject to the terms of the bailment) mere possessory title. Possessory title enables the bailee to hold their rights against third parties (so that they may sue a third party in trespass as an example). \

Similarly, and as a general rule, mere possessory title also has the logical ramification, that (unless the terms of bailment say otherwise and something like a lien is put on the goods), the bailor may regain possession at any time.

The last thing I'll say here is that the famous defence (against the following torts) of *jus tertii* (the defence essentially being, 'you can't sue me as someone else has better title than both of us') - generally never works. For example, a plaintiff with something like mere possessory title that sues a trespasser (with no title) will still be successful. This is despite a third party actually owning the goods in question (and thereby having a better title than both parties).

1 *Conversion*

Conversion refers to a situation in which the defendant handles goods (belonging to the plaintiff) in a manner mutually exclusive with the rights of the plaintiff (with respect to the goods). There is also a separate tort known as detinue (which won't be expanded upon because of its simplicity). Effectively, the tort is where the defendant does not 'hand-over' the goods (when requested) to the plaintiff who has a better title to them. Moving back to conversion, the best illustration (and leading case) of the rule is in the case of *Penfolds*.[340] In this case, the defendant (a hotelier) refilled empty bottles of wine. The bottles were owned (and labelled as being owned) by the plaintiff – a label I know and love all too well. The plaintiff sued for trespass, which failed. It failed because the plaintiff was not in possession of the goods at the time of interference.[341] In conversion however, the plaintiff was successful, with the tort not being limited towards interference with actual possession; but instead, available if the plaintiff (at the time of interference) has the *right* to possess the goods in question. Damages here (and below) are the most common form of relief.

My favourite lines come from *Penfolds*, specifically Justice McTiernan speaking about older cases:[342]

In Fouldes v Willoughby Alderson B. said, 'Any asportation of a chattel for the use of the defendant, or a third person, amounts to a conversion; for this simple reason, that it is an act inconsistent with the general right of dominion which the owner of the chattel has in it, who is entitled to the use of it at all times and in all places. When, therefore, a man takes that chattel, either for the use of himself or of another - it is a conversion.' In Burroughes v Bayne, Martin B. said that he agreed with the above statement by Alderson B.

Mr Justice Blackburn, as he was then, said in Hollins v Fowler, 'It is generally laid down that any act which is an interference with the dominion and right of property of the plaintiff is a conversion, but this requires some qualification. From the nature of the action, as explained by Lord Mansfield, it follows that it must be an interference with the property which would not, as against the true owner, be justified, or at least excused, in one who came lawfully into the possession of the goods.'

After stating certain qualifications of the statement that an asportation is always a conversion, Mr Justice Blackburn added, 'I cannot find it anywhere distinctly laid down, but I submit to your Lordships that on principle, one who deals with goods at the request of the person who has the actual custody of them, in the bona fide belief that the custodier is the true owner, or has the authority of the true owner, should be excused for what he does if the act is of such a nature as would be excused if done by the authority of the person in possession, if he was a finder of the goods, or entrusted with their custody.'

---

[340] *Penfolds Wines Pty Ltd v Elliot* (1946) 74 CLR 204.
[341] Ibid 225 (Dixon J).
[342] Ibid 234-35.

This principle would not excuse what the respondent did with the appellant's two bottles which he filled with wine which was to be delivered to his brother. This user of these bottles was inconsistent with the dominion and right of property of the appellant in the bottles; the respondent used them in his business as receptacles for the wine ordered by his brother.

2 Trespass

As above, trespass requires the actions of the defendant to interfere with a chattel, and thereby, a plaintiff who has both rights to *immediate possession,* and, who also has *actual possession* of the chattel at the time of the interference. This, again, is not necessarily ownership. That is, someone with mere possessory title may still sue in trespass. Also please note that the right to sue is not restricted through proof of loss (on the part of the plaintiff).

C *Negligence*

This is the big one. The tort has multiple components being sourced from both the common law and statute. What I will say here, as a preliminary, is that liability (under this tort) was first rather restricted. Then, beginning in the first few decades of the 20th century, the ability for a negligence claim to be successful was increased. Following this began a seemingly exponential widening of liability within this area of law until (roughly) shortly before the turn of the millennium. At which time media pressure on parliament, to restrain the common law, began to mount. The claims were bounded within a largely overinflated fear that liability, here, was becoming too expanded to be considered reasonable.

I will submit, as a preliminary, that the legislation may be argued to artificially diminish the rights of a plaintiff to receive just compensation for tortious wrongs. This is particularly true within the realm of damages calculation.

1 *Duty of Care*

The starting point in our analysis is in the determination of whether (or not) the defendant had a duty of care towards the plaintiff. This was the primary reasoning behind the historical limitations of the negligence claim - with the English legal system finding considerable difficulty in compelling members of society (without a voluntary contractual relationship) to owe each other legal duties.

Any book on negligence must begin with the seminal case - arguably the most famous English case ever; in any branch of law.

In *Donoghue*,[343] we had a patron of a café drink some ginger beer (which her friend had purchased for her). The bottle was so opaque that nobody could have seen inside. What makes the case at all relevant (for our analysis) is the presence of a decomposing snail within the bottle. The patron later found this snail (as the remainder of the drink was poured). Our plaintiff then got rather ill.

The problem here was that these types of lawsuit were ordinarily (at the time) contractual in nature. However, the plaintiff had no contractual relationship with any party (as her friend had

---

[343] *Donoghue v Stevenson* [1932] AC 562.

purchased the product). She was therefore forced into a longshot claim against the manufacturer - in negligence.

We have a whole bunch of wins and losses until the ultimate appeal to the House of Lords was initiated. Within which, the famous judgment of Lord Atkin was formulated to create the 'general duty of care.' This was prescribed as a requirement (effectively) towards the taking of *reasonable care* in avoiding acts or omissions which a *reasonable person* could *reasonably foresee* as harming those (who could be forethought as) at risk (by these actions or omissions).[344]

That's our starting point then – the general duty being to take reasonable actions to mitigate risks you (as a reasonable person) might reasonably foresee as doing harm.

That's a lot of reasonables.

There were then a whole bunch of cases which further refined the duty of care to be protective against the 'general nature of the harm' and not against exactly what was (or wasn't) experienced. Likewise, if the defendant's negligence created a dangerous situation in which a rescuer was required, and one appeared (in the following case by attempting to bring men out of a structure full of toxic fumes) – the defendant will likely have been found to have had a duty to protect these rescuers as well. That is, you not only have a duty to protect against the immediate consequences of your actions/omissions - but also against the ramifications that follow them as well. This is subject to the requirement that the rescuer did not do something completely stupid (in not caring for their personal wellbeing at all).[345]

In terms of what reasonably foreseeable actually means, my favourite case is *Haynes* whereby Lord Justice Greer gave the following description,

'It is not necessary to show that this particular accident, and this particular damage were probable - it is sufficient [to show] *if the accident is of a class that might well be anticipated, as one of the reasonable and probable results of the wrongful act.'*[346]

Notwithstanding everything I've just outlined, the *Civil Liabilities Act*[347] has now usurped the role (of the common law) and is now a definitive list of requirements (needing satisfaction) should a plaintiff aim to show that any duty of care exists. The prerequisites, for any negligence

---

[344] Ibid (Lord Atkin).
[345] *Baker v TE Hopkins & Son Ltd* [1959] 3 All ER 225.
[346] *Haynes v Harwood* (1935) 1 KB 146, 156 (Greer LJ).
[347] *2002* (NSW) s 5B (1).

claim, are almost an exact copy of those found in the common law. To be brief, these conditions are that the risk was foreseeable, not insignificant, and also that a reasonable person would have taken precautions against it.

> *(a) Mental Harm:* As you might imagine, personal or property damage are not the only two areas at risk in negligence cases. In particularly traumatic events (commonly found in car crashes as an example – but equally apply to any gruesome scene) we might also find those directly involved (or indirectly as bystanders) having mental issues developing as a result of witnessing such events. Regarding the duty of care analysis, this is the portion of the common law with which the legislation has arguably had the most to say. The requirements are now as follows:
>
> *(i) The Duty:* A person does not hold a duty to prevent another from suffering mental harm unless they foresee (or ought to have foreseen) that another person of normal mental strength may well develop a *recognised mental illness* if reasonable care is not taken.
>
> The legislation outlines circumstances which may be used to show this – such as that the mental harm suffered was from 'sudden shock,' that they had witnessed an unsightly scene, the relationship between themselves and the harmed/nearly harmed individual (or individuals), and whether there was a relationship between themselves and the defendant. Any personal injuries suffered by the plaintiff are also important factors.[348]
>
> *(ii) Pure Mental Harm:* In cases where the only harm to the plaintiff is that of mental shock, there are additional barriers which prevent recovery. These being that the plaintiff witnesses an unsightly scene or that the primary victim was a close family member to the plaintiff.[349] Again, note that there must be a recognised mental illness suffered by the plaintiff (and not simply negative/troublesome emotions).[350]
>
> *(b) Professionals:* As mentioned above, the standard of care for an ordinary defendant is that of a reasonable person. That is, would a reasonable person (in the position of the defendant) have taken the precautions?[351] For a professional, however, within the context of their giving of professional services; the standard is higher. This threshold

---

[348] Ibid s 32.
[349] Ibid s 30.
[350] Ibid s 31.
[351] Ibid s 5B.

being set at the level of what is 'widely accepted as competent professional practice.'[352] Note, widely accepted does not necessarily mean universal.[353] So, for example, in my practice as a doctor, if my actions or omissions cause another to suffer harm, I will not be found negligent unless my practice deviates from what is considered as widely acceptable Australian medical practice. This takes into account that there are often differences in how professionals would approach similar situations and/or fact patterns and that similarly competent professionals (such as doctors) may take varying degrees of actions (and sometimes different actions entirely) depending on their own experiences, their own view of the situation, and so on. Please also note that this duty of professionals to act congruently with the general standards of that profession is known as the *Bolam* principle – named after the leading case on the issue.[354] Similarly, the statutory scheme has essentially just restated the common law rules.

2 Breach

As a general principle, the rules for breach are considered met when the defendant had a duty of care (requiring satisfaction) to escape liability, and this necessary standard of care (required of this defendant) was not reached. As above, the standard is (generally) that of the reasonable person in the position of the defendant. There are really two questions present inside the leading case of *Wyong*,[355] which require answering within this portion of negligence law, for a defendant to be found liable.

(a) *Whether the Risk of Injury Exists:* The first issue is whether a reasonable person, in the position of the defendant, would have foreseen that their actions/omissions had within them a risk of injury (of some type) for the plaintiff. The determination of foreseeability is defined in a very broad manner; foreseeable risks being those risks that are 'not far-fetched or fanciful.'[356] A risk that has a very small probability of occurring, therefore, may yet be considered foreseeable, so long as it is not the creation of fantasy (or something equally far-fetched or unlikely to occur). Please also note that the statute

---

[352] Ibid s 5O.
[353] Ibid.
[354] *Bolam v Friern Hospital Management Committee* [1957] 1 WLR 582.
[355] *Wyong Shire Council v Shirt* (1980) 146 CLR 40.
[356] Ibid (Mason J).

requires foreseeable risks to be 'not insignificant'[357] for action to be required to mitigate them. It's doubtful, however, whether this change in language appreciably changes the content of the duty.

(b) *Standard of Care:* Once it is established that the risk of injury was reasonably foreseeable, the next logical question is what the reasonable person would have done to discharge their duty?

That is, what steps need to have been taken to escape liability?[358]

My favourite line, describing this, comes from Lord Reid in *The Wagon Mound*,[359]
'What that decision, in Bolton v Stone did, was to recognise and give effect to the qualification, that it is justifiable not to take steps to eliminate a real risk, if it is small and if the circumstances are such that a reasonable man, careful of the safety of his neighbour, would think it right to neglect it.'

The factors here, listed in the case above, have had additions to them from the statute.[360] These factors being:

(i) *Probability:* This is the most obvious question.
That is, how likely is the risk to materialise (should you not bother to mitigate it)?
The higher the probability of harm from the risk, the more you must do in eliminating the risk.

(ii) *Magnitude:* Should the risk materialise; how serious will the consequences be?
The more significant the possible harm; the higher the standard of care.

(iii) *Burden:* How hard is it to mitigate the risk? The harder the risk is to mitigate (for example the resources in money, time, and other factors) the less you'll be

---

[357] *Civil Liabilities Act 2002* (NSW) s 5B(1)(b).
[358] *Wyong Shire Council v Shirt* (1980) 146 CLR 40 (Mason J).
[359] *Overseas Tankship (UK) Ltd v Miller Steamship Co* [1967] AC 617 (Lord Reid).
[360] *Civil Liabilities Act 2002* (NSW) s 5B(2).

forced into doing before you've successfully discharged your duties under the law of negligence.

(iv) *Social Utility:* Is what you're doing so important to society, that the harm you create may be outweighed by other factors?

The higher the social utility, the less likely of being found liable for a breach. I've always found this rather odd. If something has such a high social utility, should we not aim to ensure it is actually done properly (thereby increasing rather than decreasing the necessary standard of care)?

So, we have a risk that has a relatively high probability of occurring, that has a high magnitude of harm should the risk materialise, that is cheap (in time and money) to prevent, and your actions don't have much societal utility. In these circumstances, you're far more likely to be found to have breached your duty of care than if any (or all) of these indicia were the other way around.

3 *Causation*

So, the defendant owed a duty of care to the plaintiff and this duty was breached; the last issue for consideration within a negligence law is whether the breach actually caused the harm claimed. The causation element can be split in twain according to the legislation[361] (being effectively a re-statement of the common law principles).

(a) But For: The negligence must be a necessary (but not necessarily sufficient) condition for the harm suffered. That is, but-for the negligence, the harm would not have occurred.

I'll give an example; I negligently drive down the road with my eyes closed and don't see you crossing. I crash my car into you. Obviously, you suffer some harm because of this. Without my negligence of not opening my eyes, you would not have been so

---

[361] Ibid s 5D(1).

injured - hence the but-for test (for negligence) test is satisfied. This (as we've seen in earlier sections of the book) is the simplest of the two inquiries.

(b) *Remoteness:* The more difficult inquiry is whether (or not) the defendant's breach should be considered so remote (from the loss suffered) that they should escape from liability.

So back to the car crash example above, let's say you break your arm in the car crash and have had a plaster cast for a period of six weeks. Upon your travelling to the medical clinic to remove the cast, you are struck by a falling branch from a nearby tree (which harms your head). On a but-for analysis alone, I (the driver of the original car six weeks ago) may well be found liable for this additional damage. This is because, but-for my initial negligence, you would not have required to go to the medical centre that day (and wouldn't have been hit over the head with the branch).

This creates a problem for causation, as no right-minded person could believe the driver of the original car is to blame for a branch hitting your head, and yet the first legal test seems to suggest so.

This daft result is tempered, therefore, with the test of remoteness; originally formulated to be the requirement that a reasonable person (in the position of the defendant) ought to reasonably foresee the subsequent type of injury (to be found liable for it).[362] Again, this foreseeability need only be towards the species of harm suffered (and not necessarily the exact chain of events). The common law remoteness test is now restated in the legislation; as referring to whether (or not) the scope of liability should extend to the harm factually caused by the defendant.[363]

My favourite illustration of the rule is found within the case of *Corr*,[364] whereby a man, subsequent to a workplace injury (very physically severe, and causing the development of depression soon after), unfortunately then intentionally jumped to his death. The predominant issues present in this case were whether the suicide was an intervening act (were the suicide a fully informed choice from a man of sound mind, there would be no question that liability would be escaped) and another question on remoteness. The

---

[362] *Overseas Tankship (UK) Ltd v Miller Steamship Co* [1967] AC 617 (Lord Reid).
[363] *Civil Liabilities Act 2002* (NSW) s 5D(1)(b).
[364] *Corr v IBC Vehicles Ltd* [2008] AC 884 (Lord Bingham).

judgment was such that the scope of liability (for consequences of the mental harm) extended to the employer in this instance and that the suicidal acts were not the actions of a fully mentally cognisant man. As such, the suicide could not be considered a *novus actus interveniens* (a new act that intervenes and hence breaks the chain of causation), and thereby, liability in negligence was founded.

The final issue which needs discussion, for causation, is that of the egg-shell skull rule. Please note that we've already discussed the rule within the criminal law section of this book – and that this analysis yields similar results. In England, the rule was formulated to be one of expanding liability, to perhaps unforeseen consequences, that were the result of the plaintiff's vulnerable peculiarities. For example, the defendant may not claim as a defence (or at least one that will work) that they should not be held liable for the broken bones of the plaintiff (say they were suffered from negligent actions at a work site) simply because the plaintiff has weak bones.[365] Effectively, the rule (probably) holds in Australia, that should the barriers to remoteness be met for a general species of harm (e.g. physical harm) then the defendant is also liable for any damages resulting from the peculiar weaknesses of the plaintiff. I say probably, here, because there is some judicial debate within the precedent, and perhaps with a different High Court (than was present when most of these issues came before it the first time), then the guiding principles may change. Notwithstanding these comments, the current state of the law, ironically, is probably still close to that of the initial New South Wales case law on this matter – with liability limited to the category of harm which was deemed reasonably foreseeable (as in *Beavis*).[366]

4 *Extra Bits of Liability*

There are a few extra titbits which need some description before we finish our analysis on liability (and how duties can be met). Above, we have spoken about the paradigm path (one well-trodden) towards a finding of negligence. Here, however, we'll speak about some peculiarities which may further guide our assessment. As a rule, we as citizens of a western liberal democracy may only be found liable for the actions in which we personally take part in.

---

[365] *Smith v Leech Brain & Co Ltd* [1962] 2 QB 405 (Lord Parker).
[366] *Beavis v Apthorpe* (1962) 80 WN (NSW) 852 (Herron CJ).

That being said, within negligence law, there are two scenarios in which this rule is broken. Please also note, these will not be detailed greatly, merely mentioned.

> *(a) Vicarious Liability:* In certain situations, if an employee of a business acts negligently and causes a third-party loss – the employer may be found liable instead of the individual employee. This may even be the case despite the employer giving warnings (against the employee) to not act in a certain way (and this 'warned about' action/inaction causes the loss).
>
> *(b) Non-Delegable Duties:* In a tangent to the above point, in certain scenarios, the duty of an organisation (or individual) to ensure that care is taken may not be delegated away to another. This naturally means that the bearers of these duties (such as an organisation/employer/individual) will always be found liable for their charge (should they suffer loss caused by negligence). These duties are generally founded in statute for professionals (such as doctors) and in professional organisations with which we hold a significant degree of trust. For example, my own previous work as a tutor within a school has shown me the litany of non-delegable duties placed upon schools as organisations (and also the individual employees within). These duties are almost invariably placed as protections on vulnerable groups (such as children) or in activities with a high 'public safety' type component.

There is one other imposition of a duty of care that we'll speak about – the statutory duty. Please note that this often overlaps with the above categories.

A statutory duty is exactly what it says on the tin. That is, a duty imposed by legislation. Most non-delegable duties are imposed in this manner. We establish negligence, here, by acting in a manner contrary to, or in failing to act in a manner consistent with, the terms of the legislation.

Legislation may be crafted this way to ensure certain professions act congruently with their mandate and also in the meeting of specific 'society wide' objectives (for example - to promote workplace safety). I've always found it odd that students learning this portion of the law can find incredible difficulty in doing so. The golden rule is to follow the damn statute – if you do this, you won't be liable (at least under the legislation). Some duties created in this manner are broad in nature - something akin to, 'thou shall have a duty of care to take reasonable steps in reducing hazards around the workplace.'

They can also be rather specific. Something like, 'in order to meet your duty of care towards your employees, thou must sing God Save the Queen before eating lunch at work.' If the wording of the statute tells you to hop on a carousel and think of England – you'll have to do exactly that (to meet your duty). There are some more detailed rules to go along with this (as developed in the courts) which may be of further use (for a more detailed study than this book provides).

5 Ways to Escape Liability

There is a whole banquet of ways to get out of liability. All of the examples we'll speak about, below, are effectively the legal implications of the statement, 'if you cock something up yourself, you lose the ability to blame someone else for the ramifications.'

> (a) *Contribo:* Contributory negligence is a doctrine whereby both the plaintiff and defendant are jointly held responsible (for the loss sustained by the plaintiff). My favourite case here (probably because Lord Denning is the judge) outlines the rule being a simple evidentiary inquiry as to whether the plaintiff indeed shares a portion of the blame for their own loss. A secondary analysis is then conducted (should the first inquiry be successful) as to the extent the damages should be reduced (that is, by how much of the loss did the plaintiff cause themselves?). The aforementioned case above, being the leading judgment of *Froom*,[367] had the plaintiff take some of the cost for losses sustained by the negligent driving of the defendant. The plaintiff caused some of their own loss because they chose to not wear a seatbelt. The judgment then went on to outline the procedure for fixing the amount of blame the plaintiff bears as that of a value judgment (a gut feeling) based on where the evidence takes you. For example, some instances have the evidence (even in similar cases) showing the negligence of the plaintiff causing more or less of their own loss; whatever the case may be. The legislation now codifies the existence of the defence[368] and gives the relevant standards of care (and knowledge of circumstances) the plaintiff is deemed to hold for themselves.[369]

---

[367] *Froom v Butcher* [1975] 3 All ER 520 (Lord Denning MR).
[368] *Civil Liabilities Act 2002* (NSW) s 5S.
[369] Ibid s 5R.

(b) *Dangerous Boredom Killers:* Should the plaintiff harm themselves while taking part in a 'dangerous recreational activity,' (e.g. a sport – definitions are present in the given reference)[370] then there will be no liability (should the loss occur from an obvious risk of the activity).[371] There are also some 'duty to warn' rules (for this category) provided by the legislation.[372]

Finally, there is a section dealing with the recreational activity's liability (as it relates to contract law). In summarised form, the section basically explains that anything written in a contract (for these activities) may modify liability however it wants to. For a more detailed explanation, the section is provided in the footnotes.[373] Also, a discussion on obvious risks will be provided below.

(c) *Obvious Risks:* An obvious risk is something that is 'risky' as a matter of common knowledge (or would have been obvious to a reasonable person in the position of the plaintiff).[374] That is, an obvious risk is something that is obviously risky (duh).
Obvious risks include those which may not be prominent or physically observable and also may have a low probability of occurring (e.g. an avalanche on a mountain side). The general rules relating to obvious risks are that the plaintiff is deemed aware of them (subject to rebuttal).[375] Similarly, knowledge of the 'species' of risk (over the exact nature) will be sufficient knowledge (to know of it).[376] There is also no general duty to warn others about an obvious risk;[377] however this is subject to the exceptions given in the section.[378]

(d) *Inherent Risks:* These are risks that cannot be avoided by exercise of skill – such as (as an unrelated illustration) your opponent (in poker) flopping (and pairing) an ace against your two kings. There is no liability imposed for the materialisations of these risks.[379] For example, a mountain guide is not liable for rocks falling on your head (this is subject

---

[370] Ibid s 5K.
[371] Ibid s 5L.
[372] Ibid s 5M.
[373] Ibid s 5N.
[374] Ibid s 5F.
[375] Ibid s 5G(1).
[376] Ibid (2).
[377] Ibid s 5H(1).
[378] Ibid (2).
[379] Ibid s 5I.

to there being no way any use of expertise or skill will avoid this outcome or minimise its effects).

D *Damages*

As a starting point, damages are formulated to place the plaintiff back into the position they would have occupied (had the civil wrong not occurred).[380] There may also be (as at common law) exemplary damages (for loss above what the initial compensatory damages would entitle). Albeit, as the name suggests, these are only available in exceptional cases (where the conduct of the defendant warrants such a measure). An example of such conduct that may enable exemplary damages to be recoverable would be some type of insult, in addition to injury, from the defendant towards the plaintiff.

My favourite paragraph detailing the rules regarding damages (for once) comes from a very recent case. In *Hassam* Lord Burrows gives a paragraph detailing the factors that the court, at common law, is to take into account when deciding the quantum of damages,

> 'In respect of PSLA in personal injury cases, it was explained by the Court of Appeal in Heil v Rankin [2001] QB 272 that the scale of values represents what the judges consider to be the fair, just and reasonable sums to award for PSLA. The determination of what is fair, just and reasonable takes into account the interests of claimants, defendants and society as a whole. The Court of Appeal also made clear that, although compensation for PSLA can never be precise, the aim is to provide full compensation.'[381]

Please note that while this case is dealing with damages relating to pain, suffering, and loss of amenity – the overarching principles remain similar for damages, more broadly, in tort law.

However, the legislation has now usurped the precedent here (and implemented its own rules within this sphere). Some academics would regard the impact on the rules governing damages to be among the most damaging (pun intended) on the operation of tort law.

Basically, the overarching objectives of the statute were to restate the common law rules (while also minimising the damages which may be available to a harmed plaintiff). For example, for economic loss (that is, damage resulting from a decrease in earning capacity – such as a

---

[380] *Livingstone v Rawyards Coal Co (*1880) 5 App Cas 25 (Lord Blackburne).
[381] *Hassam and another (Appellants) v Rabot and another (Respondents)* [2024] UKSC 11 (Lord Burrows).

successful doctor being paralysed and hence no longer able to practise) damages are limited to thrice the average state-wide salary.[382]

Also note that, similar to our assessment of 'loss of a chance damages' (in contract), any assumption on future earnings are to be calculated based off the probability that what the plaintiff claims (will come to pass) will actually occur.[383]

Any damages which are payable as a lump sum (that also include a 'future loss' component - such as for future earnings) will also have a discount rate (unless another rate is chosen) of 5% applied.[384] The legislation also removes the ability for a court to award exemplary damages in negligence.[385]

Then we have the infamous 'non-economic loss' table. Non-economic loss refers to pain, loss of life amenity, loss of life expectation, and disfigurement.[386] The table sets out the scheme for what may be awarded (under this section) by reference to the most extreme case – quantitatively.[387] So, for example, the table states that a case at severity of 16% (of the most severe case) is entitled to 1.5% of the maximum amount which may be awarded. This, of course, has led to two further questions arising in each inquiry for damages. Firstly, what is the most extreme case? And secondly, where does this case fall within the scheme? Also, make a final note that no damages are to be awarded (within this section) unless we reach (at least) 15% of the most severe case.[388] The maximum amount here is $350,000[389] and is indexed to average earnings changes.[390]

Regarding damages for plaintiffs requiring care; if the care provided is gratuitous (not paid for) then the statute also makes limitations on the payable amounts in the least severe (and even in the most severe) cases. In the least severe cases; no damages are to be awarded here (the requirement is that the plaintiff requires care for at least six months at six hours per week).[391] In the most severe cases (where care is at least 40 hours per week) the damages must not exceed the average weekly wage (of earners within New South Wales). This is despite the fact that

---

[382] *Civil Liabilities Act 2002* (NSW) s 12.
[383] Ibid 13(2).
[384] Ibid s 14.
[385] Ibid s 21.
[386] Ibid s 3.
[387] Ibid s 16.
[388] Ibid.
[389] Ibid.
[390] Ibid s 17.
[391] Ibid s 15.

carers, such as occupational therapists and/or nurses, may earn far more than the average.[392] The same calculation is true for care of less than this minimum – yet by reference to an hourly rate.[393] The limitation in the most severe cases is further presented in the 'capping off' of payment. That is, care may well be provided for 80 hours a week and yet the amount payable is still the average weekly earnings in the state. This is no different than if the care were for half that - at 40 hours.

As you can probably tell from my tone - I have *extreme* scepticism towards this statutory scheme.

E *Failures to Warn & The Therapeutic Privilege*

You'll have to forgive me for putting this portion slightly out of order.

During my Doctor of Medicine degree, one of the requirements was (and is – for every MD), to conduct a research project into an area of personal interest. My own project was a legal research paper, specifically regarding the tortious 'duty to warn' for medical practitioners and a possible exception to this requirement.

This 'duty to warn' encompasses situations where a professional (most notably a physician) is discussing the risks of a particular action with their patient. Most commonly, these cases revolve around the discussions a physician will have with their patient prior to a surgery being performed. For consent to be considered valid, the physician must discuss the inherent risks of that procedure. But to what standard is the physician held to? What risks must they divulge? What risks do they not have to divulge?

For example, if I do not tell my patient that there is an inherent risk of an allergic reaction to blood products (something that is perhaps the most obvious/common risk of this medical intervention), then I will almost certainly be (if these risks materialise) found liable, in tort, for inadequately warning my patient. Thereby, I will have negligently performed my duty, and hence damages will likely be payable for any loss suffered as a result of my inadequate warnings.

---

[392] Ibid.
[393] Ibid.

One could ordinarily think that the *standard of care* for these 'failure to warn' cases should be identical to the general duty of care for professionals. Namely that as long the professional's warnings are congruent with widely accepted medical practice in Australia – they will have discharged their duty.

They would, however, by wrong in thinking this.

The standard in these types of cases is slightly different; being by a two-tiered test under the leading judgment of *Rogers*.[394]

The facts of *Rogers* were that a patient was discussing the risks of a particular ophthalmological procedure with their doctor. The patient was blind in one eye and the doctor was proposing to perform a procedure on that same eye. It came with an unavoidable, but *very* low risk (less than one in ten thousand), of causing blindness in the other eye (and hence total blindness for the patient). The doctor did not warn the patient of this. Unfortunately, while the procedure was performed with good care and skill, the unavoidable complication resulted – causing total blindness. Was he negligent in failing to warn the patient of this?

Under the old *Bolam* standard, by reference to contemporary practice, he would not have been found negligent – as it was considered widely accepted within Australian practice to not require full warnings of every single complication (especially not *really* rare ones such as the complication suffered) that could possibly arise from a procedure.

However, under this new case, he was found negligent - as the court instituted a new test for these types of cases. In professional warnings, the new two-tiered standard is that the professional is required to,

(a) *Objective:* Tell the patient everything that an ordinary patient, in the patient's position would like to know, AND,

(b) *Subjective:* To warn of risks that they know (or ought to reasonably know) that this *particular patient* would want to be informed of.[395]

---

[394] *Rogers v Whitaker* (1992) 175 CLR 479.
[395] Ibid.

Please also note that causation, in these 'failure to warn' cases, is whether the court is satisfied (at the balance of probabilities standard) that the patient would *not* have gone ahead with the procedure had they been given adequate warnings.[396]

Rogers also mentions an exception to this requirement, namely that in certain cases, it may not be in the patient's best interests to tell them of the risks associated with a certain procedure – and hence the physician may not have a tortious duty to tell them. This is the so-called *therapeutic privilege*. Within *Rogers,* the duty of a physician to disclose a material risk may be narrowed via a reasonable belief (on the part of the doctor) that such a disclosure would be damaging to the individual patient before them,[397] such as where the patient is unusually nervous, disturbed, or volatile.[398]

Other Australian cases have also dealt with this issue and may provide illustrations of where the privilege may apply. Please note that the following list of Australian/foreign cases comes essentially directly (some minor rewording) from my medical school research paper.[399]

> (a) *Saxon*: The Western Australian Supreme Court determined that the privilege did not, without more, extend even to a *very anxious* patient.*[400]* As such, more than simple anxiety (even if severe) is required for the privilege to arise.
>
> (b) *DiCarlo*: The Queensland Court of Appeal concluded that 'general practices' of doctors, in withholding warnings, without considering the effect on *individual* patients, could not give rise to the privilege.[401] That is, doctors are under an obligation to assess each individual patient, for their particular peculiarities, before any claim of therapeutic privilege may be successful.
>
> (c) *Haylock:* The privilege could not arise in respect of an emotionally mature/reasonable man.[402]

---

[396] *Chappel v Hart* (1998) 195 CLR 232, 246; *Wallace v Kam* (2013) 250 CLR 375, 383-84.
[397] *Rogers v Whitaker* (1992) 175 CLR 479, 486-90.
[398] Ibid 490.
[399] Stephen George Prorellis, *A Systematic Review of Therapeutic Privilege – Developments in the Anglo-Australian Law & Proposals for Future Healthcare Policy* (Doctor of Medicine, University of Notre Dame Australia, 2023). As a side note - I worked for hours uncounted on this research paper; I'd rather my favourite sections get used in this book rather than sitting idly in the university's electronic file cabinet.
[400] *Teik Huat Tai v Saxon* (1996) WASC 1.
[401] *Di Carlo v Dubois & Ors* [2004] QCA 150 [78]-[81].
[402] *Haylock v Morris and Anor* [2006] ACTSC 86 [29].

(d) *Battersby:* The claim of privilege <u>was successful</u> in denying liability, in failing to warn of material risk, where the patient was suffering from acute depression and had a high risk of suicidality.[403] While this case was before *Rogers*,[404] it's central reasoning has not yet been overturned. As such, this case may showcase what level of patient impairment (creating a possible detriment in receiving health information pertaining to risk) may give rise to the privilege.

In terms of foreign caselaw on the subject (again - essentially directly from my paper):

(a) *Canada:* The leading case, of *Reibl*, decided that the privilege to withhold information may exist where the patient is 'unable to cope' with the information.[405]

The decision of *Meyer* then stated that the privilege could not be considered part of the Canadian common law.[406] However, due to its position within a lower court, it is/was unable to overturn *Reibl*.

The later decision of *Pittman*, also within a lower court, reiterated that the privilege was indeed part of the law. However, the court held that it did not apply to the specific facts of a patient with depression, in the context of a physician not taking sufficient measures to ensure the patient's emotional state prevented them (and would undoubtably cause harm) from receiving the information.[407]

(b) *England and Wales: Sidaway* found that the privilege may arise whereby a physician makes a *reasonable* assessment that the disclosure of risk may cause a serious threat of psychological damage to the patient.[408] *Chester* then limited this ability via stating that only 'wholly exceptional' cases may fall into this category.[409]

The most recent leading case of *Montgomery,* however, moved the legal position in England (to warn of material risk) away from *Bolam*,[410] and towards something closer to the Australian case of *Rogers* (and it's two tiered test; with both objective and subjective limbs - as assessed above).[411] This being said, the court specifically mentioned that the privilege may arise where

---

[403] *Battersby v Tottman* (1985) 37 SASR 524, 527.
[404] (1992) 175 CLR 479.
[405] [1980] 2 SCR 880, 114 DLR (3d), 895.
[406] *Meyer Estate v Rogers* (1991), 2 OR (3d) 356, 366.
[407] *Pittman Estate v Bain* (1994), 112 DLR (4th) 257, 399-400.
[408] *Sidaway v Board of Governors of the Bethlem Royal Hospital* [1985] AC 871 (Lord Scarman).
[409] *Chester v Afshar* [2004] UKHL 41 [16].
[410] *Bolam v Friern Hospital Management Committee* [1957] 1 WLR 582.
[411] *Rogers v Whitaker* (1992) 175 CLR 479.

a physician reasonably considers that the disclosure may cause serious harm to the patient;[412] wording very similar to the original scope illustrated by *Sidaway*.

(c) *United States:* This case found that the privilege is *'carefully circumscribed'* where *'risk-disclosure poses such a threat of detriment to the patient as to become unfeasible or contraindicated from a medical point of view.'*[413] This is my favourite decision on the subject.

I think the most we can say about this subject is that while the courts, in principle, are willing to countenance a departure from the tortious requirement of warning patients of all material risks – they are unlikely to do so in individual cases unless the fact patterns are truly exceptional. Similarly, one thing which I have not mentioned, at all, in this section on tort law thus far (or at all in my medical research paper) is that the spectre of insurance almost certainly has impacted the development of the law. Most of the time, it is not the individual defendant that pays for tortious liability – it is their insurance company. With the development of insurance as an industry – tort law has similarly expanded into areas where liability did not previously intrude into. This is perhaps felt most acutely in the area of professional indemnity, whereby, essentially all payouts for negligence will be borne by the relevant insurance agency and not the individual professional.

---

[412] *Montgomery v Lanarkshire Health Board* [2015] UKSC 11 [87]-[88].
[413] *Canterbury v Spence* (1972) 464 F.2d 772, 789.

IX You Get The Government You Deserve

I wish to finish the academic portion of the book off, by speaking, rather quickly, about what government (here I am referring to the legislature and executive) does in bettering the lives of citizens. Since the catastrophe of the Global Financial Crisis, I feel that people have picked up exactly the wrong impression of government. Perhaps cynicism has overtaken optimism regarding the good which may be achieved. Perhaps apathy regarding the political process has only increased (to the point of putting our bets on precisely the wrong horses).

Now I'm not saying governments don't cock it up on occasion, admittedly somewhat routinely, too routinely. Notwithstanding these comments, the ability for policy to improve lives cannot be overstated. How many individuals are better off in Australia (and not bankrupt - or worse) since the passing of universal healthcare coverage, or the age pension, or the litany of other social programs which ensure the duties we should all feel to each other (in a civilised society) are met. The source of the increasing negative opinion, felt by the populace regarding government, I feel, can be summarised in the following two areas.

1 *Unrealistic Expectations*

Despite what someone on the progressive/socialist left may tell you, government can never fix everything ailing a society. Policy, I would submit, is there only to 'set the rules of the game' and in the positioning of a basic social safety net. Post these objectives, with some extra goodies as well (like a defence force – the most crucial role of government), the rest is up to individuals, within a free society, to chart their own destiny. I would argue that the more any government attempts to intervene, beyond this mark, the more harm that comes out of this intervention. Every time a government attempts to wrap its citizens in cotton wool - it usually causes more ill than good. So, the next logical question is what exactly does 'rule setting' and a 'social safety net' entail? Just note that this entire chapter is mere opinion, with my (aforementioned) political economics book discussing these issues with far more detail than what is available here.

> *(a) Rule Setting:* Ensuring that there is a sufficiently resourced court and accompanying enforcement regimes (such as tribunals) to carry out the law during the course of civil

and public disputes. This also requires coupling with regulatory bodies (with oversight from elected representatives and the judiciary) with whom regulatory power on commercial standards are vested (within the bounds set by statute). There is an obvious balancing act, here, of empowering (or not) of these executive bodies. The more ability they have in curbing standards – the less scope for the private market to operate (for good or evil). Every regulation should ideally have a cost-benefit analysis undertaken, to ensure it is not, on aggregate, detrimental to the wider community. There should also be, as a general rule, a presumption against regulation at all.

(b) *Social Safety Net:* Included here are the basic direct payment systems, such as unemployment or age-related pensions. These systems operate as to care for citizens, who would not (but-for these services), have the ability to provide for themselves.

Included in the social safety net are also indirect assistance programs - which aid the promotion of equality of opportunity (such as education and health care). This past year (over many, many years in fact) I've heard some real garbage on the topic of healthcare, particularly in the debates within the United States. The main issue of contention, against universality, effectively boils down to the claim that one cannot have both universality and high-quality care at the same time (within the same system). While this argument may seem initially attractive – it does not consider the possibility of structuring the healthcare marketplaces (plural), in tandem, to support both objectives.

The healthcare market is like any other, with both suppliers and demanders. Suppliers produce at increased quantity as the price goes up and demanders buy more of something as the price decreases. The only difference, here, is the increased inelasticity of the demand curve (as people will buy the medicine that they need regardless of price).

Everyone up to equilibrium in a free-market system receives healthcare, with each supplier having a corresponding demander. Post this mark, sick citizens who cannot afford care will not receive it (as there is no profit in healing poor people who cannot purchase it). Ensuring these individuals are covered through a public system leaves the private incentives unchanged (and actually provides for a baseload return to suppliers operating in this market). However, keen eyed readers will note that I've assumed the public system does not cannibalise the incentives of the private market – this is only the case if certain prerequisites are met.

The first prerequisite is that (contrary to every socialist ever) there still needs to be a private market. Similarly, everyone who can afford their own healthcare needs to be included in this market as to ensure the profit incentives (and hence the innovation incentives) are maintained. The public system should, therefore, only be a safety net for those who cannot afford their own coverage. Similarly, to remove the 'free-rider' problem (of those who can afford their own healthcare but forego it and choose to remain in the public system) – there needs to be a mandate of some sort to ensure this does not happen. A simple tax levy (as done in Australia) upon individuals above a certain income (who do not purchase their own insurance) does the trick here. If the levy is larger than the cost of private insurance – almost everyone will buy their own insurance.

It is for this reason I am not in favour of a solely public system – retaining the profit incentive is necessary to ensure continued innovation. I would therefore submit that the two-tiered system of Australia, with two parallel healthcare markets, is the ideal model (with the private system valuing quality and the public ensuring universality).

There are also other issues requiring discussion as well; regulatory bodies that are empowered to curtail price gouging, a balanced patent system, and other requirements of a competitive market (such as price transparency rules). That being said, we'll leave this discussion here for now.

2 *Apathy*

Even with these benefits pointed out, some will still feel the urge to claim that the (not uncommon) governmental cock up is due cause for 'checking out' of the system all together. I have heard too many times (and from too many people), something to the effect of, 'government sucks anyway, so why bother?'

I would propose that this is a mistake for only one reason. No matter how much you personally care, we will still have a government. Would you prefer their actions to be scrutinised or not?

A sure-fire way in ensuring governments do not care about you is to similarly not care about what it does. The title of this chapter is that people get the governments they deserve (naturally, I am speaking on aggregates here). Should the people vote for a monster, they have only themselves to blame. Should they vote for a stupid monster, again, the only item with the ability to conjure up who is responsible, is a mirror.

Government is hard, it's tricky, it involves compromise (messy compromise in which neither side gets exactly what they want). I would submit that we need to move beyond the absolutism of the current age, an era where compromise on both sides is despised. Instead, I would argue, we need to shift towards a more shared future in which we are all more valued, where cock ups are recognised immediately, and fixed (instead of pretending they aren't there). Naturally, there is an exception for any proposition that is in the non-negotiable category. Something like the taking away of rights to free speech. Then, of course, the only way out is to fight (and keep fighting) till your last breath.

I would humbly submit, with all my meagre 21 years on this earth as evidence; that if we all were more informed about what our governments were doing and cared more deeply about their actions – the quality of all governmental decisions would vastly improve. Similarly, should we not vote in a manner compatible with maximising the public good – we get representatives that don't hold those objectives as paramount either (perhaps holding their own interests above that of their constituents).

As a later edit, I'm 26 now, and I still believe this – for whatever that's worth.

Building on this point, should we continue to vote for those who give us easy answers to complex problems – we will only end up with the exact shallow populism that we have today.

When the answer to something as complex as tax reform is presented as just lowering rates (without dealing with the network of deductions) we end up with inequality (between those with the resources to afford an army of accountants and lawyers and those without such means).

When a politician is successful in feeding on the dark desires within our own hearts, like the character in some medieval fantasy TV show, we all falter. We owe it to ourselves, to our children, and all those who have come before. We need to do better, to be better. We need to be greater than the sum of our parts. We need to leave this place better, healthier, and more together than how we found it.

I will use a typically American phrase (within their founding document) to summarise my position. We as citizens have a collective and unbreakable duty to ensure that we bequeath a more perfect union than the one we inherited.

As some more later edits – I'm now nearing my 28th birthday. Time flies. The only thing I will add to what I've already written here is that scepticism of government is a natural occurrence when people feel they have been left out of the decision-making process – and people have been feeling that a whole lot recently. The bubble around the government class has gotten thicker – nigh impenetrable. The media certainly has its fair share of blame here too. The media landscape has become infected with sensationalism, a certain vapid quality, and (in my mind the most damning) a complete loss of grace and understanding that we live in a fallen and fundamentally imperfect world.

Every time there is some tragedy the media is then quick to point and blame. Every time some unfortunate circumstance occurs – there will be an inevitable and unending chorus of voices that ask for government to tighten the noose around human freedom. Create some new regulation, pass some new law, spend some more money (that we don't have) here or there, limit judicial discretion in a manner unthinkable even a few years ago, alter the court process (or rules of evidence) for certain types of litigation, and on and on it goes. Misquoting statistics, making stuff up, and sometimes just pain lying. The bias (sometimes even from public institutions that are bound to impartiality) is palpable.

The worst of it, however, has got to be the limitations we've seen placed on free expression – particularly on the internet.

So-called 'misinformation' has become a magic word for any government or legacy media institution that wishes to clamp down upon the ability for critics of the current regime to do so.

For example, now have open regulators of the internet (under the guide of internet 'safety') in most Western countries. This was unimaginable even a few years ago.

We cannot have a functional democracy if anytime someone says something that is controversial, they are then shut down. The way our system functions is that good ideas triumph over bad ones – and we don't know which ideas are good or bad from the outset. There is a contest, sometimes a heated contest, between ideas. For this to occur there needs to be an allowance for all ideas, even the bad ones, to be put forth into the public square. People have the right to make fools of themselves in the public domain. I want to know who the idiots are. I equally want to know who I can't show my back to. I certainly don't want to be coddled by a government that thinks it knows best – aided by a legacy media that wants to squash its upstart competitors.

The best disinfectant for bad ideas is sunlight. Let the sun shine down upon them.

X BIBLIOGRAPHY

A *Articles/Books/Reports*

J R R Tolkien, *The Lord of the Rings* (HarperCollins Publishers, 15th ed, 1995)

Stephen George Prorellis, *A Systematic Review of Therapeutic Privilege – Developments in the Anglo-Australian Law & Proposals for Future Healthcare Policy* (Doctor of Medicine, University of Notre Dame Australia, 2023)

.

B *Cases*

Aberdeen Railway Co v Blaikie Brothers (1854) 1 Macq 461

Abdallah v R [2016] NSWCCA 34

Adelaide Company of Jehovah's Witnesses Incorporated v Commonwealth (1943) 67 CLR 116

Allcard v Skinner (1887) 36 Ch D 145

Allen v Pierce (1895) 3 Terr LR 319

Angell v Duke (1875) LR 10 QB 174

Associated Newspapers Ltd v Bancks (1951) 83 CLR 322

Associated Provincial Picture Houses Ltd v Wednesbury Corporation [1948] 1 KB 223

Australian Broadcasting Corporation v Lenah Game Meats Pty Ltd (2002) 208 CLR 199

Australian Conservation Foundation Incorporated v Commonwealth (1979) 146 CLR 493

Australian Woollen Mills v Commonwealth (1954) 92 CLR 424

Bainbrigge v Blair (1839) 48 ER 1032

Baker v TE Hopkins & Son Ltd [1959] 3 All ER 225

Bateman's Bay Local Aboriginal Land Council v Aboriginal Community Benefit Fund Pty Ltd (1998) 194 CLR 247

Battersby v Tottman (1985) 37 SASR 524

Beavis v Apthorpe (1962) 80 WN (NSW) 852

Benedetti v Sawiris [2014] AC 938

Bennett v Wyndham [1862] 4 De GF & J 259

Bettini v Gye (1876) 1 QBD 183

Biotechnology Australia Pty Ltd v Pace (1988) 15 NSWLR 130

Boardman v Phipps [1966] UKHL 2

Bolam v Friern Hospital Management Committee [1957] 1 WLR 582

Bratty v A-G for Northern Ireland (1963) AC 386

Breen v Williams (1996) 186 CLR 71

Bristol and West Building Society v Mothew [1998] Ch 1

British Movietonews Ltd v London and District Cinemas Ltd [1952] AC 166

Byrnes v Kendle (2011) 243 CLR 253

Canterbury v Spence (1972) 464 F.2d 772

Carlill v Carbolic Smoke Ball Co [1893] EWCA Civ 1

Chaplin v Hicks [1911] 2 KB 786

Chappell & Co Ltd v Nestle Co Ltd [1960] AC 87

Chappel v Hart (1998) 195 CLR 232

Chester v *Afshar* [2004] UKHL 41

City and Westminster Properties Ltd v Mudd [1959] Ch 129

Clarke v Dickson (1858) 120 ER 463

Coco v A N Clark (Engineers) Ltd [1969] RPC 41

Codelfa Construction Pty Ltd v State Rail Authority (NSW) (1982) 149 CLR 337

Commercial Bank of Australia v Amadio (1983) 151 CLR 447

Commonwealth v Barry (1878) 125 Mass. 390

Con-Stan Industries of Australia Pty Ltd v Norwich Winterthur Insurance (Australia) Ltd (1986) 160 CLR 226

Corr v IBC Vehicles Ltd [2008] AC 884

Crabb v Arunn District Council [1975] EWCA Civ 7

D & C Builders Ltd v Rees [1965] 2 QB 617

Darby v DPP (NSW) (2004) 150 A Crim R 314

Dawson v Clarke (1811) 18 Ves 247

Derry v Peek [1889] UKHL 1

Devaynes v Noble (1816) 35 ERf 767

Di Carlo v Dubois & Ors [2004] QCA 150

Donoghue v Stevenson [1932] AC 562

Dowsett v Reid (1912) 15 CLR 695

Dowse v Gorton [1891] AC 190

DPP v TY (2006) 167 A Crim R 596

Dunlop Pneumatic Tyre Co Ltd v New Garage & Motor Co Ltd [1915] AC 79

Durham Holdings Pty Ltd v New South Wales (2001) 205 CLR 399

Erlanger v New Sombrero Phosphate Co (1878) 3 App Cas 1218

Ermogenous v Greek Orthodox Community of SA Inc (2002) 209 CLR 95

Fagan v Metropolitan Police Commissioner [1968] 3 All ER 442

Falcke v Gray (1859) 62 ER 250

Federal Commissioner of Taxation v Vegners (1989) 90 ALR 547

Fink v Fink (1946) 74 CLR 127

Fletcher v Bealey (1885) 28 Ch D 688

Foran v Wight (1989) 168 CLR 185

Foskett v McKeown [2001] 1 AC 102

Fowler v Fowler (1859) 4 De G & J 250

Freeman and Lockyer v Buckhurst Park Properties (Mangal) Ltd [1964] 2 QB 480

Frost v Northern Beaches Council [2022] NSWSC 1214

Haylock v Morris and Anor [2006] ACTSC 86

Gibson v Manchester City Council [1979] 1 All ER 972 294

Gillard v The Queen (2014) 88 ALJR 606

Giumelli v Giumelli (1999) 196 CLR 101

Goodman v Harvey (1836) 4 A&E 870

Goss v Chilcott [1996] AC 788

Green v Daniels (1977) 13 ALR 1

Hadjiloucas v Crean [1988] 1 WLR 1006

Hadley v Baxendale (1854) 156 ER 145

Haoui v R (2008) 188 A Crim R 331

Hassam and another (Appellants) v Rabot and another (Respondents) [2024] UKSC 11

Hawkins v Clayton (1988) 164 CLR 539

Haynes v Harwood (1935) 1 KB 146

He Kaw Teh v The Queen (1985) 157 CLR 523

Hely-Hutchinson v Brayhead Ltd [1967] 1 QB 549

Henderson v Merrett Syndicates Ltd [1995] 2 AC 145

Hili v The Queen (2010) 242 CLR 520

Hogg v Kirby [1803] EngR 513

Hong Kong Fir Shipping Co Ltd v Kawasaki Kisen Kaisha Ltd [1962] 1 All ER 474

Hospital Products Ltd v United States Surgical Corporation (1984) 156 CLR 41

Hot Holdings Pty Ltd v Creasy (2002) 210 CLR 438

Household Fire and Carriage Accident Co Ltd v Grant (1879) 4 Ex D 216

Hoyt's v Spencer (1919) 27 CLR 133

Interfoto Picture Library Ltd v Stiletto Visual Programmes Ltd [1987] EWCA Civ 6

James Roscoe (Bolton) Ltd v Winder [1915] 1 Ch 62

JC Williamson Ltd v Lukey and Mulholland (1931) 45 CLR 282

John Alexander's Clubs Pty Ltd v White City Tennis Club Ltd (2010) 241 CLR 1

Kauter v Hilton (1953) 90 CLR 86

Kelly v Copper [1993] AC 205

King v Jones (1972) 128 CLR 221

Kioa v West (1985) 159 CLR 550

Kirk v Industrial Court of New South Wales (2010) 239 CLR 531

Knight v Knight (1840) 49 ER 56

L'Estrange v F Graucob Ltd [1934] 2 KB 394

Lange v Australian Broadcasting Corporation (1997) 189 CLR 520

Laird v Pim (1841) 151 ER 852

Letterstedt v Broers (1884) 9 App Cas 371

Libertarian Investments Ltd v Hall [2013] HKCFA 93

Lindsay Petroleum Co v Hurd [1874] LR 5 PC 221

Lister v Romford Ice and Cold Storage Co Ltd [1957] AC 555

*Livingstone v Rawyards Coal Co (*1880) 5 App Cas 25

Loftus v Roberts [1902] 18 TLR 532

Mabo v Queensland (No 2) (1992) 175 CLR 1

Malik and Mahmud v Bank of Credit and Commerce International SA [1998] AC 20

March v E & MH Stramare Pty Ltd (1991) 171 CLR 506

Markarian v The Queen (2005) 228 CLR 357

McCloy v New South Wales (2015) 257 CLR 178

McPhail v Doulton (1971) AC 424

Meyer Estate v Rogers (1991), 2 OR (3d) 356

Meyers v Casey (1913) 17 CLR 90

Midland Bank Plc v Wyatt [1997] 1 BCLC 242

Minister for Arts, Heritage and Environment v Peko-Wallsend (1987) 15 FCR 274

Minister for Immigration and Citizenship v Li (2013) 249 CLR 332

Minister for Immigration and Multicultural Affairs v Jia (2001) 205 CLR 507

Montgomery v Lanarkshire Health Board [2015] UKSC 11

Morley v Morley (1678) 22 ER 817

Murrumbidgee Groundwater Preservation Association Inc v Minister for Natural Resources [2005] NSWCA 10

Muschinski v Dodds (1985) 160 CLR 583

Musumeci v Winadell (1994) 34 NSWLR 72

National Trustees Executors and Agency Company of Australasia Ltd v Barnes (1941) 64 CLR 268

Nelson v Dahl (1879) 12 ChD 568

Nolan v Collie & Merlow Nominees Pty Ltd (In Liq) (2003) 7 VR 287

Nottingham University v Fishel [2000] EWHC 221 (QB)

NWL Ltd v Woods [1979] 3 All ER 614

Nydam v The Queen [1977] VR 430

Octavo Investments Pty Ltd v Knight (1979)

Olley v Marlborough Court Hotel [1949] 1 KB 532

Onus v Alcoa of Australia Ltd (1981) 149 CLR 27

O'Rorke v Bolingbroke (1877) 2 App Cas 814

O'Sullivan v Management Agency & Music Ltd [1985] 3 All ER 351

O'Sullivan v R; Flanders v R; Tohu v R & NRH v R [2012] NSWCCA 45

Overseas Tankship (UK) Ltd v Miller Steamship Co [1967] AC 617

Overton v Banister (1844) 3 Hare 503

Papadimitropoulos v The Queen (1957) 98 CLR 249

Parker v McKenna (1874-75) LR 10 Ch App 96

Patel v Ali [1985] 1 All ER 978

Penfolds Wines Pty Ltd v Elliot (1946) 74 CLR 204

Pharmaceutical Society of Great Britain v Boots Cash Chemists (Southern) Ltd [1953] 1 All ER 482

Pittman Estate v Bain (1994), 112 DLR (4th) 257

R (Abbasi) v Secretary of State for Foreign and Commonwealth Affairs, Ex parte Abbasi [2003] UKHRR 76 CA

Radford v De Froberville [1977] 1 WLR 1262

Raftland Pty Ltd as trustee of the Raftland Trust v Commissioner of Taxation (2008) 238 CLR 516

Raffles v Wichelhaus [1864] EWHC Exch J19

Re Bosworth (1889) 58 LJ Ch 432

Redgrave v Hurd (1881) 20 Ch D 1

Re French Caledonia Travel Service Pty Ltd (In Liq) (2003) 59 NSWLR 361

Regal (Hastings) Ltd v Gulliver [1967] 2 AC 134

Re Hallett's Estate (1880) 13 Ch D 696

Re Harvard Securities Ltd [1997] EWHC Comm 371

Reibl v Hughes [1980] 2 SCR 880, 114 DLR (3d), 895

Re London Wine Co (Shippers) Ltd [1986] PCC 121

Re Tempest (1866) 1 Ch App 485

Richardson v Mellish (1824) 2 Bing 229

Robinson v Harman (1848) 1 Ex Rep 850

Rogers v Whitaker (1992) 175 CLR 479

Rowland v Divall [1923] 2 KB 500

Royal Botanic Gardens and Domain Trust v South Sydney Council (2002) 186 ALR 289

*Royall v The Queen (*1991) 172 CLR 378

RTS Flexible Systems Ltd v Molkerei Alois Muller GmbH & Co KG [2010] UKSC 14

R v Blaue (1975) 61 Cr App R 271

R v Brown [1994] 1 AC 212

R v Burstow; R v Ireland [1998] 1 AC 147

R v Cairns [1999] 2 Crim App Rep 137

R v Cheshire [1991] 1 WLR 844

R v Crabbe (1985) 156 CLR 464

R v Delk (1999) 46 NSWLR 340

R v Falconer (1990) 171 CLR 30

R v Filipetti (1984) 13 A Crim R 335

R v Fuge (2001) 123 A Crim R 310

R v Jones [1987] Crim LR 123

R v Katarzynski [2002] NSWSC 613

R v Kirby; Ex parte Boilermaker's Society of Australia (1956) 94 CLR 254

R v Kitchener (1993) 29 NSWLR 696

R v M'Naghten (1843) 8 ER 718

R v Savage; DPP v Parmenter [1992] 1 AC 699

R v Taktak (1988) 14 NSWLR 226

R v Tolson (1889) 23 QBD 168

R v Velumyl [1989] Crim LR 299

R v Whyte [2002] NSWCCA 343

Ryan v Mutual Tontine Westminster Chambers Association (1893) 1 Ch 116

Ryan v The Queen (1967) 121 CLR 205

Saunders v Vautier (1841) 49 ER 282

Scally v Southern Health and Social Services Board [1992] 1 AC 294

Sidaway v Board of Governors of the Bethlem Royal Hospital [1985] AC 871

Simpkins v Pays [1955] 1 WLR 97

Smith v Clay (1767) 29 ER 743

Smith v Leech Brain & Co Ltd [1962] 2 QB 405

Snook v London and West Riding Investments Ltd [1967] 2 QB 786

Somerset v Stewart (1772) 98 ER 499

South Australia Asset Management Corp v York Montague Ltd [1997] AC 191

Speight v Gaunt [1883] UKHL 1

State of New South Wales v Ibbett (2005) 65 NSWLR 168

Stewart v Ronalds (2009) 76 NSWLR 99

Stylk v Myrick (1809) 170 ER 1168

Tasmanian Conservation Trust Inc v Minister for Resources (1995) 55 FCR 516

Teik Huat Tai v Saxon (1996) WASC 1

The Commonwealth v Verwayen (1990) 170 CLR 394

The Federal Republic of Brazil v Durant International Corporation (Jersey) [2015] UKPC 35

The King v Anna Rowan – A Pseudonym [2024] HCA 9

The Medina (1876) 2 PD 5

The Moorcock (1889) 14 PD 64

Tierney v King [1983] 2 Qd R 580

Toll (FGCT) Pty Ltd v Alphapharm Pty Ltd (2004) 219 CLR 165

Tuberville v Savage [1669] EWHC KB J25

Twinsectra Ltd v Yardley [2002] 2 AC 164

Ultraframe (UK) Ltd v Gary Fielding & Ors [2005] EWHC 1638

Vallance v The Queen (1961) 108 CLR 56

Victoria Park Racing and Recreation Grounds Co Ltd v Taylor (1937) 58 CLR 479

Wallace v Kam (2013) 250 CLR 375

Walters v Woodbridge (1878) 7 Ch D 504

Waltons Stores (Interstate) Ltd v Maher (1988) 164 CLR 387

Warman International Ltd v Dwyer (1995) 182 CLR 544

Wayne v Boldiston (1992) 62 A Crim R 1

Way v Latilla [1937] 3 All ER 759

Western Australian Insurance Company Ltd v Dayton (1924) 35 CLR 355

Williams v Roffey Bros & Nicholls (Contractors) Ltd [1989] EWCA Civ 5

Wilson v The Queen (1992) 174 CLR 313

WN Hillas & Co Ltd v Arcos Ltd [1932] UKHL 2

Wong v The Queen (2001) 207 CLR 584

Worrall v Harford (1802) 8 Ves 4

Wright v Atkyns (1823) Turn & R

Wyong Shire Council v Shirt (1980) 146 CLR 40

B *Legislation*

Bail Act 2013 (NSW)

Chancery Amendment Act 1858 (UK) 21 & 22 Vict. C 27

Civil Liabilities Act 2002 (NSW)

Commonwealth of Australia Constitution Act 1901 (Cth)

Competition and Consumer Act 2010 (Cth)

Crimes Act 1900 (NSW)

Crimes (Sentencing Procedure) Act 1999 (NSW)

Evidence Act 1995 (NSW)

Mental Health and Cognitive Impairment Forensic Provisions Act 2020 (NSW)

Native Title Act 1993 (Cth)

Sale of Goods Act 1923 (NSW)

Slavery Abolition Act 1833, 3 & 4 Will 4, c 73

Supreme Court Act 1970 (NSW)

Trustee Act 1925 (NSW)

C *Other*

New South Wales Bar Association, *'Media Release: Consent Proposals Could Result in Significant Injustice,'* (Web Page, 26 May 2021) <https://nswbar.asn.au/the-bar-association/publications/inbrief/view/08b347d11316f1372f3414b4c466afe4>

www.ingramcontent.com/pod-product-compliance
Lightning Source LLC
Chambersburg PA
CBHW031926240526
45464CB00023B/1717